▲ pop open here ▲

YOU'RE
AWESOME

Gourmet
Leadership

Dear Teri,

   As you continue to lead the
RFH in 2022, may this book serve
to light / ignite your "secret sauce!"
   Enjoy and Take Care,

                                    — March 2022 —

Advance Praise

"Carolyn Maue is an experienced leadership coach that has helped hundreds of people realize their potential with pragmatic, action-oriented support. I am one of them. In *Gourmet Leadership*, she makes those enduring insights fun and accessible through her own special sauce."

Dale Whittaker, PhD, Lead Senior Program Officer
at Bill & Melinda Gates Foundation,
Higher Education Champion and Strategist

"Carolyn Maue serves up an epicurean feast for those looking to hone their leadership skills into a fine art. A mix of the perfect ingredients to develop your own leadership style awaits you in this helpful new book."

Diane Holder, President/CEO,
UPMC Health Plan, Inc.

"I've worked with Carolyn Maue on and off for sixteen years during my university presidency. Her new book, *Gourmet Leadership*, is the perfect recipe for any leader looking for new guidance or a refresher on leadership development. Carolyn's own secret sauce is her simplicity—her ability to genuinely connect with leaders using simple language and examples to address the complex issues associated with leadership."

Paul Hennigan, EdD, President Emeritus,
Point Park University

"Carolyn Maue is an exceptional professional coach and mentor. Carolyn easily identifies critical underlying growth opportunities that express as professional performance issues. In her caring and sophisticated approach, she consistently facilitates the personal, as well as professional, growth of her clients. Sharing her approach is a gift to us and our organizations."

Clay Marsh, MD, Vice President and Executive Dean Health Sciences,
West Virginia University

"Talk about secret sauce! Carolyn's unique blend of leadership expertise, writing style, and culinary passion cook up a compelling metaphor for igniting passion and purpose in leadership. Carolyn expertly weaves together leadership frameworks, practical tools and strategies, personal stories, and a soupçon of humor to make this work a recipe for success for leaders at all levels. Bravo for *Gourmet Leadership*!"

Ann Bowers-Evangelista, PsyD, MBA,
Fortune 500 Leadership Consultant and Executive Coach,
Endurance Leadership Expert

"Like a skilled chef, Carolyn combines phenomenal ingredients—her experience, storytelling and research—with an innovative recipe to create something new and delicious. *Gourmet Leadership* shares insights and best practices that are immediately accessible and applicable to real-world situations. Carolyn has created a truly revelatory and entertaining book."

Grant J. Heston, Vice President for University Relations,
Virginia Commonwealth University and the VCU Health System

"Like my well-worn cookie recipe book, Carolyn Maue's *Gourmet Leadership* will become a dog-eared manual I turn to for advice on coaching and developing exceptional leaders. Sprinkled throughout this book are nuggets of simple wisdom and stories that leaders can apply immediately with their teams to reach their organizational vision."

Pamela Nabors, President and Chief Executive Officer,
CareerSource Central Florida

"Just as she has done teaching and coaching countless people toward leadership success, Carolyn Maue has taken an incredibly creative approach in *Gourmet Leadership* and made understanding the secrets of leadership relatable and fun . . . or, perhaps I should say 'delicious.'"

Roger Pynn, APR, CPRC, Senior Counsel,
Curley & Pynn—The Strategic Firm®

"Given its fresh insights and original recipes for leadership success, *Gourmet Leadership* is a book to devour. It's a unique perspective on how to use mental models from the gourmet cooking world and apply them to the world of business leadership. A delicious feast!"

Chris Fehrnstrom, Executive Coach,
Former Chief Marketing Officer of Constellation Brands

"Every new leader has the potential for success and satisfaction in work and life. Carolyn's life work and her new book are about helping identify those ingredients that will ensure success and satisfaction in deep and meaningful ways. My time with Carolyn helped change my life. Let this book do the same for you."

Nelson Chipman, EdD, Assistant Vice President,
Point Park University Online

"What a breath of fresh air! Carolyn Maue's *Gourmet Leadership* is just what the chef ordered for leadership development. I haven't had as much enjoyment in reading a book about change and leadership since *Who Moved My Cheese* and *Switch*. Carolyn is masterful in defining Gourmet Leadership and the ingredients to be an effective leader. Having known Carolyn for over twenty years, I see a lot of Carolyn's careful insight and wisdom in her words as she explains leaderships skills that are essential in today's world."

Crystal McCormick, MS, Higher Education, DEI Professional,
Global-Career Development Facilitator

"Tantalizing teachings await you in *Gourmet Leadership*! As someone who has trained under Carolyn Maue through my time serving in leadership positions with the Florida Public Relations Association, I was thrilled to find that her expert knowledge in growing leadership skills and presence has been perfectly captured within the pages of this book. Not only does Maue beautifully fold insights on leadership in with clever stories and analogies from the culinary world, but she also provides real tools and exercises that help the reader actively participate in exploring his or her own areas of opportunity and leadership growth. I can't wait to fully unlock my own 'secret sauce!'"

Alyson Sologaistoa, APR, CPRC,
FPRA State Past President

Gourmet Leadership

Turn up the heat
on your secret sauce!

CAROLYN MAUE

Gourmet Leadership

Turn up the heat on your secret sauce!

© 2021 Carolyn Maue

To contact the publisher, Gravitas Press, visit www.GravitasPress.com

ISBN : 9781735943558

Content coach and publisher: Bonnie Budzowski

Cover & Interior Design by: Melissa Farr, melissa@backporchcreative.com

GRAVITAS PRESS

Dedication

"For the chefs and cooks whose pots continue to simmer,
no matter what their kitchen."

Contents

Author's Note

When I started writing this book several years ago, I had long been inspired by chefs and restaurateurs and wanted to integrate that inspiration into this book. I never imagined that by the time the book was finished, the world would have been gripped for nearly two years by the COVID-19 pandemic. For me, one of the most painful experiences of the pandemic has been realizing the impact on restaurateurs, chefs, and their staff. I have had great concern about the welfare of these individuals, their future, and the long-term state of the restaurant industry. I missed the experience of going to restaurants, tasting interesting food, and interacting with fascinating chefs and wait staff.

Many restaurants temporarily closed; some for good. It has been a time of great upheaval, uncertainty, economic instability, and grief. I watched many do the best they could to keep going, displaying immense perseverance, courage, and creativity. Now as we are all emerging into a new era, we are watching as some flounder and some flourish.

My hope going forward is for creativity and success to grow once again in restaurants, large and small. With renewed appreciation for their talents and contributions, may we join together to support the inspirational chefs, staff, and restaurateurs as they navigate a new, and hopefully flourishing, frontier.

Acknowledgments

This book has been simmering for a long time. Pamela Fischer, the talented creativity and leadership coach and founder of Motivity, convinced me I could serve it up to the world. I'm grateful for the tools, templates, and heaping platefuls of encouragement Pamela provided. Penny Tavarez supported the project early on, introducing me to Alice Julier, PhD, whose wisdom and knowledge of the history of cooking and cookbooks informed my perspective. Successful business writer Suzanne Caplan provided guidance and perspective. Roger Pynn generously read an early draft cover to cover, providing insight, suggestions, and support, for which I am indebted. Chris Gent generously made promotional videos for the book through our collaboration in Florida Public Relations Association.

My special thanks to the chefs, restaurateurs, and food experts who graciously agreed to be interviewed and quoted for this book: Chef Alison Negrin, Sherree Goldstein, Armani Ghrissi, Chef "Chaz" Smith, Domenic Branduzzi, Chef Neall Bailey, Dana Cowin, Mark Becker, and Jessica Flinn. Their amazing stories and points of view make the leadership concepts sizzle.

Bonnie Budzowski, the amazing book coach, collaborator, and principal at Gravitas Press, brought insights, wisdom, encouragement, and knowledge and assured this book came to light. I am forever changed and grateful.

My virtual assistant extraordinaire, Joyce Kane, brought her steadfast, eyes-wide-open approach to the editing process and supported me in navigating unknown waters of the book world. Graphic designer Melissa Farr's creative eye brought the text to life with her cover design and graphics.

This book is truly a stew of concepts, ideas, and knowledge I have gained over decades of working at the intersection of human behavior and the workplace. Several colleagues contributed specific knowledge to the book. Peter Rubin, MD, MBA, FACS, Chair of the Department of Plastic Surgery at the University of Pittsburgh, generously shared his methods for delegation to teams. Joel Garfinkle, a leader and knowledge expert in executive coaching, graciously allowed me to reference his material on leadership presence.

Through my leadership coaching practice, I have been inspired by, and learned so much from, the many leaders with whom I have collaborated. Their example of courageous and innovative leadership informed this book. These leaders include, but are not limited to, Paul Hennigan, EdD, Robert Behler, Grant Heston, Nelson Chipman, Clay Marsh, MD, Ellie Monaco, Leeann Cerimele, and Maribeth Ehatz, PhD.

I have been buoyed and inspired by the generosity of my colleagues in the Alexcel Group—The Alliance for Leadership Excellence. Nancy Parsons introduced me to Bonnie Budzowski and inspired me with her own writing, publishing, and business acumen. Simon Vetter and Chris Fehrnstrom, through their unabashed excitement for the book's concept, cheered me on at a pivotal point, fueling my energy to keep going. Ann Bowers-Evangelista, PsyD, Barbara Mintzer-McMahon, Colleen Bastian, PhD, Val Markos, PhD, Maya Hu-Chan, and Lisa Walker, PhD, provided unwavering encouragement and valuable suggestions.

The love and encouragement of friends and colleagues fueled the fire. Carol Bennett contributed her honest wisdom, and the inspired title *Gourmet Leadership*. Bonnie Artman Fox, Lynda Stucky, Rosemarie Perla, Dee Giffin Flaherty, PhD, Jill Gordon, Nina El-Tobgy, Gay Fogarty, PhD, Judy Stoddard, Karin Kaser, Eileen Swazuk, Jay Morgan-Schleuning, Joan Haley, and Dick Finnegan supported me with boundless enthusiasm for this project. My son, Rob Taylor, and daughter, Sarah Hunt, contributed perspective and insight from their real-world leadership experiences. My sister, Deborah Maue, contributed the same, along with a dose of unwavering belief in me.

My husband, Bryan Hunt, provided boundless love, support, and encouragement. He is now, and always will be, the chicken in my soup, the apple in my pie, and the chocolate in my cake.

 *Introduction*

Welcome to Gourmet Leadership

Allow me to take you to dinner. Walk with me into a beautiful restaurant—a top-tier establishment with white tablecloths and candles, the kind of place that seems to twinkle. We are greeted warmly by the host and escorted to our reserved table where we are comfortably seated. We catch a whiff of something delectable and aromatic coming from the kitchen, which leads to giggles of anticipation. Then, we take in the calm, nuanced surroundings and settle in for what we know is going to be a very special experience.

This is an example of a gourmet dining experience, to be sure, but gourmet is not always about white tablecloths and candlelit rooms. It can be applied to more than just a restaurant or cuisine. It's about best-in-kind experiences. Wouldn't it be great if every time you went out for a meal—be it a diner with the best eggs and bacon, a local mom-and-pop joint with your favorite fried chicken and greens, a well-loved little pizza joint, or a romantic seafood place by the water—you had a best-in-class experience? Every morsel would be delicious, every encounter pleasant, and each meal a memorable experience. That's gourmet!

Gourmet most often refers to the world of food and drink, the expensive and elaborate, yet it also can describe a person who strives to be of exceptionally high quality, bringing a unique specialization to his or her work—a person who is a connoisseur, with discriminating taste, and who appreciates subtleties.

As a lover of food and wonderful dining experiences, as well as an executive leadership coach, I have been as inspired by professional achievements created by organizational leaders—some at the highest executive levels, and some not—as I have by dining experiences created by talented restaurateurs and executive chefs. For years,

I have explored and tested out how these two worlds intersect and overlap; this book is the result.

WHAT IS GOURMET LEADERSHIP?

Gourmet leadership is leading at a level that will delight and inspire your direct reports, your superiors, your peers, and your customers, and help you find joy in dishing up your best, in service to others. As you bring your best to your role, you ultimately change your team, department, organization, and community for the better—one person, one dish, one project at a time. In short, this book is about helping you become the best you can be so you can bring out the best in your team members.

Think about the intricacy of gourmet food preparation. Every dish is the result of the head chef's unique approach to envisioning it: finding the freshest ingredients, assuring those ingredients are prepared effectively (cooked at just the right temperature for the right amount of time), and pleasingly presented.

This level of excellence is not easy to achieve, whether you are leading in a restaurant, a hospital, or a company. Most leaders need help learning how to support their teams to achieve at this high level. In fact, because there is not a standardized way of preparing leaders, the skills of most leaders are often like Swiss cheese—filled with holes. That's where my expertise comes in. In this book, I will fill those gaps by providing tools and techniques that can immediately be applied, quickly escalating your leadership effectiveness.

You don't have to be in the restaurant industry to be a gourmet leader. You can learn to escalate your leadership to the gourmet level, quickly mastering the fundamentals of leadership, while adding what makes you unique—your "secret sauce" that makes your leadership its finest. *Gourmet Leadership* will help you become the most amazing chef you can be in whatever "kitchen" you are in.

DEVELOPING A LEADERSHIP PLAN

This book lays out the fundamental ingredients of gourmet leadership. As you consider each ingredient, you'll look at examples for "Cooking It Up." You'll escalate your leadership effectiveness by learning and applying these ingredients to your real-world experience. By the time you reach the end of the book, you'll have worked through a series of exercises that will help you cook up a personal developmental plan, which will encompass the following:

- ☙ A compelling, clearly articulated vision for success for yourself and your team
- ☙ A strengths based approach that identifies and leverages innate and developed strengths
- ☙ A shift from "doer" to leader, in mindset, behaviors, and habits
- ☙ A culture of delegation and development of your direct reports
- ☙ A well-functioning team that has clear goals and corresponding responsibilities
- ☙ A culture that expects and maximizes conflict and change
- ☙ An ability to delight and inspire others with your leadership presence

Your success at leading yourself, leading others, and leading the organization depends upon your utilization of these "ingredients." But there is another important element that will elevate you to the level of a gourmet leader—your "secret sauce."

TURNING UP THE HEAT ON YOUR SECRET SAUCE

The house specialty in many restaurants features the chef's secret sauce. In its literal sense, a secret sauce is all about cooking. It's what distinguishes one chef from another. The recipe for the sauce is usually a closely guarded secret because it's the component that creates the magic in a chef's signature dish.

Gourmet leaders cook up a dish of leadership competencies and flavor it with their secret sauce—the personal strengths and talents that set the best leaders apart, adding energy, momentum, inspiration, and often, a whole lot of fun. Think, for example, about Sheryl Sandberg, Steve Jobs, and Barack Obama—leaders renowned for doing big jobs and making unique contributions, each in his or her special style. These leaders draw others to themselves because they know and leverage their own secret sauce. Successful leaders all have a secret sauce, and when a leader has developed the fundamental skills of leadership and knows how to leverage his or her secret sauce, things sizzle.

What exactly do I mean by secret sauce? Secret sauce is what makes a leader memorable. It's what makes you you. It's often fueled by interests or hobbies, like sports, or music, or gardening. It's a comfort level and a love of something that is part of your identity. Your secret sauce is a combination of your strengths, experiences, passions, and perspectives. It's your unique flavor that sets you apart from others.

These different, sometimes quirky experiences and talents may include a bit of whimsy. I worked with a distinguished executive leader who always wore socks with Disney characters on them. Secret sauce can add delight, fun, and interest. It's also most likely what adds to your happiness. It's something to be embraced, celebrated, and leveraged to get the job done, all while enriching the experience of working with you. When you bring it to your leadership at work, you bring your whole self. And that creates energy, interest, variety, and trust. Once you identify your secret sauce, you can be creative, adding interesting, different ways of looking at things, spicing things up, and honing your leadership essence.

My dentist of many years displayed photos of himself golfing with professional football players. During dentistry procedures, I was pleasantly distracted by images of this skinny, white, balding little man surrounded by towering, smiling African American athletes. His secret sauce was on display, and that's what I remember most about him.

Secret sauce can be an effective communication tool, inviting people into informal discussions about that art on your wall, the photos of your soccer team, that music you are playing, the smell of the cookies that you baked that are sitting on your desk. It invites conversation. And that naturally leads to building trust.

When your secret sauce is on display, the message is, "Here I am!" and it is magnetic. Others want to know more about you. What's so great about it is that it gives the people around you permission to bring their secret sauce to work too.

My secret sauce has been brewing and bubbling for over thirty years of collaborating with leaders in creating successful and flourishing workplaces. My sauce, like yours, has simmered over time, integrating my strengths, interests, and experiences into a flavorful mix. It is based upon my belief, endowed to me by my mother from an early age, that each person is unique. I remember her telling me as a little girl, "There is no one in the world quite like you." This belief has stewed throughout my life and work, guiding me in my path to assist others in becoming the best they can be. It fuels my interest and passion for seeing the differences in each person and helping others achieve their heart's desire by using their own special talents, passions, and views on life. Since I am also a singer, writer, cook, and baker, I am apt to bring in stories and anecdotes from these creative aspects of my life that illuminate a point or shed a different light. I bring my love of life to my love of people—that's my secret sauce.

Whether I'm talking with a client about a growth strategy, a challenging project, a conflict between members of a team, a funny moment, or an insight, I want to bring a spark to every conversation that allows people to be themselves as individuals while also seeing something bigger and better that will contribute positively to the world.

One of my leadership coaching clients loved to walk at his lunch break, fueling his fascination with architecture and the sights and sounds of the city. When he became president of an urban university, he used his knowledge and love of the neighborhoods, alleys, nooks, and crannies in developing the university's strategic plan, which focused on expanding the footprint of the university, making it an anchor of the downtown district. This is using secret sauce at its best—to create a better organization, community, and world through talents and interests that come naturally.

Chef Negrin's Secret Sauce: Truth in the Material

Chef Alison Negrin has been a food industry pioneer in bringing healthy and sustainable foods to a variety of tables. Chef Negrin's early experience included being a line cook in Alice Waters's groundbreaking restaurant Chez Panisse. She has been an executive restaurant chef, a culinary instructor, and a consultant on bringing healthier foods to organizations. She recently consulted as the R&D chef for a startup that designs robots that are deployed in vending machines in hospitals, colleges and universities, and grocery stores with prepared salads and bowls that the chefs create. In addition to her leadership in sustainability, Chef Negrin prepares and teaches cooking as an art. She is currently consulting on opening a restaurant in Berkeley, California.

Chef Negrin explains:

I studied art, specifically sculpture, in college. There came a point when I had to decide what to do going forward. I saw my choices as pursuing a Master of Fine Arts or going to culinary school. Because I was not sure I would be good enough as an artist, I chose culinary school. I thought, "Okay, I'll study culinary arts and become a chef, and then I can do my art on the side." Eventually I learned that cooking IS an art.

My cooking and presentation have been influenced by art and travel. There's a term in art called "truth to the material" in which you have to consider the innate qualities of the material you are using, whether it be a piece of wood or rock, and create something that is natural and appropriate. In cooking, this means allowing a vegetable or fruit to be what it's going to be.

My cooking has been influenced by my travels. In Japan, I found the sense of minimal design appealing. In Denmark, where I lived for about five years, I became interested in sustainability without really realizing it. I was fortunate to live there with a host family who grew all their vegetables, cut wood for heat, hunted, fished in the rivers for fresh eel, and used every part of the hog they received from their uncle's farm. Most wonderful was that I learned to prepare the food from all of this bounty. I was in heaven.

My cooking has been influenced by my love for beauty. I just love beautiful vegetables. When cooking in the restaurant, I would go to the farmer's market and see what was in season and ask myself, "Okay, what's the best way I can cook this? What culture should I think of when I'm using this particular vegetable?"

I love cooking with fire, so I enjoy grilling and roasting things at a very high temperature. I also enjoy cooking low and slow, using the braising technique, which involves taking an inexpensive cut of meat and enhancing the cooking process with aromatic vegetables, herbs, and a really good stock. Eventually, the piece of meat that is very sinewy and tough becomes soft with all of the flavor in it.

DEVELOPING CAPACITY IN OTHERS

No matter how talented, a chef cannot run a restaurant alone. Much of what gets done, from food preparation, to serving, to adjusting the lighting in the restaurant, is done by others. That leads us to a basic premise of leadership and this book: your most important job as a leader is to develop others. Whatever your industry, be it a service industry, manufacturing, technology, higher education, or healthcare, this is true. Unless you are a business of one, developing and utilizing others is essential to delivering services and goods. It is also critical to building capacity and innovation.

All businesses need to be constantly building capacity to keep pace with trends and find solutions to increasingly complex problems; in short, to stay innovative and relevant. You are only one person, with give or take 175 hours this month to accomplish the goals of your department/division/organization. To reach those important goals, it is critical that you invest time and energy to building the capacity of your team. This is the only way to perform at your highest and deal with the endless pivots required in this world of constant change.

This book will help increase your leadership effectiveness as you develop your team members and lead your team. As you learn and apply the ingredients in this book, you'll increase your ability to mobilize your team so that your organization can continue to change, grow, and innovate as needed. Additionally, these ingredients and exercises can be used by your team members for their own development, so feel free to pass them on!

WHAT TO EXPECT FROM THIS BOOK

Each chapter represents an ingredient in the recipe for gourmet leadership, identified and refined through my interactions with executives as a leadership coach. When learned and leveraged, that ingredient will escalate your leadership. Mix the ingredients together and "cook them up," and you'll be at the level of gourmet leadership.

⚜ **Ingredient #1: Plan the Feast! Your Compelling Vision** guides you to identify your personal vision as a leader—what kind of leader you want to be, how you want to lead others, and where you want to take them. From there, you'll build a strategic vision with the input of the team, clarifying the mission, gathering essential information, composing a vision statement, and designing a work plan to get there. In Chapter 1, you'll work your way through thought-provoking exercises and activities, culminating in a step-by-step recipe for a visioning retreat you can plan and lead for your team.

⚜ **Ingredient #2: Strengths . . . Your Magic Ingredients** emphasizes that effective leadership focuses on strengths rather than weaknesses. For many of us, this requires a shift in thinking. Strengths based leadership is also about bringing out the strengths in others. In Chapter 2, you'll identify your innate strengths (ones you've had since you can remember), your manifested strengths (ones you have used and honed over time), and the leadership competencies that come easily to you as well as ones you need to develop.

✤ **Ingredient #3: Is This Too Spicy? Feedback and Understanding Perceptions of Your Leadership** provides a road map for getting and giving feedback, a practice critical to leadership success. In Chapter 3, you'll explore the connection between feedback and a growth mindset. You'll also discover specifics on what and who to ask for feedback and how to use what you learn. You'll uncover suggestions for creating a feedback culture and being a role model for feedback.

✤ **Ingredient #4: Sous Chef to Executive Chef . . . Your Transition from Doer to Leader** is about the essential transition from individual contributor to leader. Making this transition starts with shifting your activities and focus from doing the work to one of overseeing and assuring it is done consistently well. This shift requires changes in attention, responsibilities, and habits, and is a challenging and crucial step in assuring your success as a leader. Therefore, it involves managing your mood, tasks, and energy. In Chapter 4, you'll have an opportunity to create a plan to manage these dynamics in your evolving role.

✤ **Ingredient #5: Chop! Chop! Chop! Getting Things Done through Others** focuses on establishing a win/win culture of mutual responsibility through accountability and delegation. Chapter 5 provides step-by-step guidelines for delegation conversations that set clear expectations for results while also supporting growth of staff members. You'll discover a replicable accountability model, including a path to establishing roles, goals, and timelines. You'll have the opportunity to apply an accountability model to real-world situations.

✤ **Ingredient #6: The Right Cookware . . . Your Best Team** identifies the elements of successful teams, including team trust, good team conflict, commitment to team, accountability to one another, and attention to results. Chapter 6 provides information to identify and build each of these essential elements. It also walks you through a clearly delineated process for a team retreat, complete with objectives, agendas, and action steps to move a team from mediocre to successful.

✣ **Ingredient #7: Hot Tamales! Dealing with Difficult People** provides tools for creating a culture that accepts and deals with conflict while keeping a cool head when things get hot in the kitchen. I describe my 7 C's for working with difficult people; examples include changing your questions, finding courage to stop avoiding, being clear on what needs to change, and utilizing the power of conversation. Chapter 7 includes steps to apply these 7 C's in your own challenging situations, and how to reduce the impact of those "hot tamales!"

✣ **Ingredient #8: Pièce de Résistance . . . Your Leadership Presence** provides tools and tips for identifying and utilizing your personal style to build your leadership presence. Essential elements of leadership presence include gravitas, effective communication, and professional appearance. Chapter 8 provides a personalized leadership presence assessment tool and describes opportunities to link leadership presence with your secret sauce. You'll explore how to use various elements of leadership presence to your advantage in different situations.

As I explain each ingredient in the recipe for gourmet leadership, you'll learn about it in a broad sense and then complete practical exercises to make that ingredient your own. The exercises in each chapter will help you to taste and cook with that ingredient. Each chapter will help you apply what you already bring to this topic, as well as fresh learnings to quickly increase your leadership effectiveness, a key goal of this book. As you work your way through these pages, you'll be encouraged to discover and include your own secret sauce.

As you learn and apply these ingredients to your challenges and add your secret sauce, you'll gradually turn up the heat on your leadership by making more conscious decisions about the best ways to lead and achieve your goals. You'll then consciously be able to decide how to add your special flavor to the day-to-day tasks of leadership—lending your authentic self to the success of your team and your organization.

────── COOKING IT UP: RECIPES FOR SUCCESS! ──────

Once you have read about each leadership ingredient, you'll be able to follow and complete the steps in each Cooking It Up section, which provides the recipe for applying that leadership ingredient to your own situation and challenges. And with each ingredient, you'll have the opportunity to reflect on how you can turn up the heat on your secret sauce.

The following components will be in each Cooking It Up section:

 Mise en Place. Mise en place provides the opportunity to explore your mindset about each chapter's ingredient, assessing any need to shift in ways that prepare you to increase your effectiveness.

 Steps to Use the Ingredient. Exercises in this section provide opportunities to apply each chapter's ingredient to your own situation and challenges.

 Add Your Secret Sauce. Your secret sauce, in essence, is what makes you memorable. People will be drawn to you, will connect to you, and have confidence to follow you, when you know what your secret sauce is and use it wisely.

 Tastings—Tidbits for Your Team. This section provides suggestions and strategies for using the ingredient with your team members to escalate their leadership too!

Mise en Place

Mise en place, pronounced *meez-ahn-plahss*, is a French cooking term which means "put into place." This term refers to having all of your ingredients prepared and ready to use in your dish before you begin cooking. When chopped vegetables, spices, and all the other ingredients for a dish are laid out in little containers, handy at a moment's notice, the chefs call this "mise en place."

The term has a much broader meaning then just preparing ingredients or gathering ingredients in advance of cooking. Writer and chef Dan Charnas uses the concept of mise en place as a philosophy and system for what chefs believe and do, even going so far as to call it an "ethical code." In the kitchen, the phrase is used as a noun (e.g., the setup of the array of ingredients), a verb (e.g., the process of preparing), and a state of mind. All of these uses, however, refer to someone who knows how to be well prepared.

In our leadership kitchen, think of mise en place as the opportunity to shift gears, think about the importance of an ingredient in your leadership, and develop a productive mindset about an ingredient. This will prepare you to apply an ingredient to your leadership style using the recipe steps that follow.

Add Your Secret Sauce

Your secret sauce, in essence, is what makes you memorable. People will be drawn to you, will connect to you, and have confidence to follow you, when you know what your secret sauce is and use it wisely. Throughout this book, you'll be encouraged to think about ways you can use your secret sauce. Here are some ways to identify it:

- ☙ What are you most interested in?
- ☙ What makes time fly by when you are doing it?
- ☙ What metaphors come to mind when you are problem-solving? Animals? Cars? Numbers? Sports? Food?
- ☙ What are you talking about when people pay the most attention to you? What do you write about?
- ☙ What are you thinking about when your eyes glisten?

Tastings—Tidbits for Your Team

Each Cooking It Up section will have suggestions on how you can apply that chapter's ingredient in your interactions with your team, whether it be helping them design and implement a vision, identify and utilize their strengths, adopt effective ways to get feedback, or increase their leadership presence.

HOW TO USE THIS BOOK

Have fun with this book! You can start with Ingredient #1 and work your way through sequentially, completing the Cooking It Up sections as you go. Alternatively, you can utilize the ingredients that are most important to you and push past ones that are not as urgent right now. Better yet, pass those sections along to one of your team members who can use that information and hone that skill. Most importantly, take note of where you shine, what excites you, and where you feel lighter—that's your secret sauce in the exciting, challenging, mystifying art of leadership!

I recommend that as you move forward through this book, reading the stories, the concepts, the advice, and completing the exercises, you continually work to apply them as specifically as you can to what you are experiencing in the very moment you are reading. This book will only be helpful if you can apply what you learn in practical ways. For example, the vision you develop today is based on what you know now, in a time of clarity or upheaval, and it could change. But it's what you know *now*. The strengths you use during a time of crisis, such as the COVID-19 crisis we are just coming out of, may be somewhat different than those you use in less turbulent times. You must trust that what you are learning and doing now will be beneficial to you in the future, laying the foundation for different challenges and opportunities, whatever the future holds.

Gourmet leadership is the combination of skill and creativity that all great head chefs and all great leaders have. It's the ability to inspire, engage, and develop others to get things done the right way, using the excellence, flavor, and style of that individual's unique approach—his or her secret sauce. That's what this book is about—helping you to become the high quality, specialty leader that you are!

For more resources from
Gourmet Leadership: Turn up the heat on your secret sauce!
and downloadable copies of leadership ingredients and recipes go to:
www.gourmetleadershipbook.com

Plan the Feast!
Your Compelling Vision

Look around you—at the room you are in, the building, the street, and even the neighborhood or town. These things did not always exist, and you were not always where you are now; the buildings, streets, job, life, and role you have now were non-existent for you in the past. Chances are, for at least part of your current reality, you had a vision of the life you are now living. You imagined it. You saw it, or part of it. It was not yet real, but it was forming in your mind. Some part of you longed for something else—perhaps a better job, more responsibility, greater autonomy, or a chance to make more of an impact. And your vision—that longing, that sense of wanting more—led you to where you are now.

Congratulations! You made this happen. You are here at this moment in your life because you envisioned it.

Now think about your favorite restaurant. Did it appear on the scene recently or is it a reliable, entrenched establishment in your neighborhood? Is it top-tier or a favorite lunch place? What do you love about it? A special dish? The ambiance?

The restaurant you are imagining did not, of course, appear out of thin air. A restaurateur had a unique vision, maybe of a bustling pizza joint, an authentic French bistro in a quiet setting, or a quick lunch stop for organic salads and soups. This personal vision—the type of food, the staff needed to run it, the equipment, the cost, even the type of customer to attract—eventually evolved into a strategy to make your favorite restaurant a reality. The restaurateur's initial vision was the start of the process of making that restaurant come to life.

This process of envisioning is a combination of spontaneity, ingenuity, creativity, and planning. Without a clear idea of where you want to go, who you want to be, or what you want to "cook," your creative longing will not come to full fruition.

Vision is a fundamental ingredient of great leadership. It is foundational to team success. In any organization, a vision leads a team forward to the next endeavor or next phase—The Next Big Thing. Great leaders know, and are fueled by, their vision for the future. And it's that sense of forward motion which naturally entices others to follow. Without it, teams and organizations can flounder and lose enthusiasm for the future.

Your vision, like that of a great chef's, will be comprised of what you want to create, how you want to create it, and the type of leader you want to be. As a leader, you are not only living in the now, you are also building your future. Your vision will be a touchstone for you and those around you as you complete your day-to-day work, navigating changing and conflicting priorities. It starts with who you are, your unique purpose in the world, and your mix of strengths, experiences, and passions (aka: your secret sauce). Your vision will serve as a beacon for where you're going and what's possible.

As a leadership coach, I continue to be amazed by the varied visions that leaders develop to change the world: I've worked with a brilliant surgeon who strove to design procedures heretofore unheard of in modern medicine; I've supported a university president as he imagined revitalizing a section of a city while educating an increasingly diverse student population; and I've watched a facilities director inspire a team to ensure a 100 percent safety record. (It was a privilege to celebrate with her when they reached it!)

IDENTIFY YOUR PERSONAL VISION

At this point, you might be muttering, "I have no idea what my vision is. I am too busy, I have too many things to think about, and I barely know what I'm doing tomorrow, let alone what I'll be doing five years from now." Believe me, I understand. Unfortunately, most work cultures do not provide much room or time for visionary thinking.

You might also be thinking that your organization has already defined its vision, mission, and values. Maybe that vision is even written on a poster on your office wall. That is great, but not enough. Your personal vision is an essential element of your secret sauce, conveying where you passionately want to go. You need to know and be able to articulate your individual vision and how it supports the vision of the organization.

Your vision for yourself starts with your honest description of how you see yourself several years from now. It answers these questions:

- ❦ Where do I want to go?
- ❦ What do I long to do?
- ❦ What comes next?

Sometimes a vision can build on what you are already doing, taking it up a notch, making it bigger, deeper, or richer. Other times, a vision can be a spark of an idea that will not go away or keeps returning. A vision can also be informed by identifying an opportunity to provide, create, or do something innovative and new. It should always be grounded in your strengths, what you love to do, and what excites you.

I bet you have some inklings of your vision, even if they are not fully developed. Here are some key questions you can ask yourself to more fully develop your vision:

- ❦ If I woke up five years from now, completely fulfilled and joyful, what would I be doing?
- ❦ When have I been happiest in the past? What elements of that time can I take into the future?
- ❦ What am I doing now that would bring me more fulfillment if I could do it even more successfully?
- ❦ What strengths of mine fuel my vision?
- ❦ What gap am I uniquely qualified to close?
- ❦ How can I fuel my vision with my secret sauce?

This ingredient of leadership, identifying your personal vision and articulating it to your team, is not only important for you as an individual, but also fundamental to the success of your team. It's the first step toward getting you and your team heading in the same forward-looking direction, fueled by enthusiasm and passion, and it will escalate your effectiveness. It should be ambitious as it will have a huge influence on the decisions you make.

Leaders sometimes skip the stage of creating a personal vision. Allowing yourself to envision a different or better future than what you currently have takes courage and requires a belief in yourself. Some leaders may think that, because they work for an organization, their responsibility is to develop a strategic vision in alignment with the company. But without a meaningful personal vision as a foundation, a strategic vision rings hollow. People don't follow a strategy—they follow you. And you are in a leadership role because of your experience, talent, strengths, ideas, and passion for where you and your team can all go together. Your vision will ignite their fire. Together you can then figure out how to achieve it, strategically.

In the Cooking It Up section of this chapter, you'll have the opportunity to clarify your vision statement so that you can articulate it to others, an important ingredient in the recipe for gourmet leadership.

Restaurateur Sherrie Goldstein's Secret Sauce: Creating a Comforting Space

Restaurant owner Sherree Goldstein had a vision for her neighborhood restaurant, Square Café, in Pittsburgh, Pennsylvania. After seventeen successful years, Square Café, which serves fresh local food in a friendly environment that brings the community together, continues to thrive. Sherree's vision to live beautifully came to life while overcoming adversity and family resistance.

Chef Goldstein says:

> I grew up in a family business in manufacturing and textiles in which everyone worked all the time. Everything was hard, including the taxes, the employees, and the hours. My mom basically worked 9 a.m. to 9 p.m., just about every day, including weekends.
>
> In my early twenties, I went to rehab for a drug and alcohol problem. Two years after I got sober, I began to work at the rehab facility. I ended up working there for twelve years. During those years, I had a vision of opening

a little pastry and coffee shop with an art space in which customers could relax and just hang out. While it seemed a pipe dream, I knew this was the next thing for me. It felt right. When I shared my plan with my mom, with whom I am close, she told me the café would ruin my life. It was a roadblock in our relationship until a few days before the café opened. Mom came to see the café and was blown away by what she saw.

As soon as we opened, our sales skyrocketed. I think it's because we have a good vibe at Square Café. It was important to me to build an environment and culture that created space for people to come and feel safe and comfortable. And to feel loved. That remains my ultimate goal.

ENGAGING THE TEAM: EXPANDING A PERSONAL VISION TO A STRATEGIC VISION

Once you've identified your personal vision, it's time to get your team involved in fleshing out a strategic vision for the group. Here is an effective process:

- ❦ **Clarify the mission.** Articulate what the department is currently doing as the foundation for where they want to go in the future.
- ❦ **Gather essential information strategically.** Identify internal and external factors that will be critical to formulating and reaching an achievable vision.
- ❦ **Compose a strategic vision for the future.** Articulate the vision to serve as a beacon going forward for the entire team.
- ❦ **Formulate a workable action plan.** Generate a plan with specific steps, responsibilities, and deadlines to achieve the vision.

Miguel, a world-renowned surgeon, researcher, and author in his mid-40s, came to me for coaching. The surgeries he had perfected literally saved and altered his patients' lives. Happily married with several children, close to his parents and siblings, Miguel was also a leader in national professional associations. He led a research lab that was making cutting-edge contributions to its field, and he was a mentor to countless medical fellows, residents, researchers, and students.

Despite the value he was bringing to individual patients and the contributions in his field through research, Miguel had longed to have an even greater impact. He wanted to build his medical group's capacity to solve complex problems and help even more patients and families than they currently did. He knew if he was going to do that, he needed to accept the position of department chair in the university health system, overseeing the sixty-plus physicians and the managers, researchers, and other professionals who supported them. He accepted the position to make a greater contribution to his profession.

Miguel said, "I have a vision. I want this to be the best department for this kind of surgery, in the world." He was clear about his personal vision. His biggest challenges were getting others to buy into his vision and then formulating a process to define the steps and responsibilities to achieve it. He wanted to get his team members energized and excited so his vision could be transformed into a strategic vision for his team, one they could all embrace and own. Miguel knew that involving each member of a loosely configured group of doctors in this vision was essential to success. It would also help his team evolve into a cohesive one, working collaboratively to create synergy.

Miguel introduced his desire to formulate a vision with key physicians in one-to-one conversations and in team meetings. He emphasized the need for the team to work together to move from the current state to even more success in the future. He emphasized the need for a defined process. Miguel got key physicians' and managers' buy-in to participate in a series of meetings specifically focused on clarifying the department's strategic vision and identifying the steps needed to get there. We agreed that he would follow the process outlined below:

Clarify the Mission

Most organizations have a formalized mission statement describing the "what" and the "how" of that organization. This statement describes what the organization does and what sets it apart from the competition. The how includes the goals, ethics, culture, and values. Engaging a team in developing a strategic vision begins with a careful review of the organization's stated mission.

Appropriately, Miguel and the team discussed the department's mission and values in the context of the larger hospital at length. They agreed that the department's mission could be encapsulated in this way:

Our exceptional surgeons restore health through state-of-the-art, research-based procedures.

Gather Essential Information Strategically

In an article on Forbes.com, Jack Zenger, one of the founders of the field of leadership development, described the steps leaders can take to increase strategic vision by performing targeted research:

- ❦ **Spend time with customers and clients.** Understand how these stakeholders think and what they would like to have that is currently not available. Review the current state and what is already in place, and understand the organization, its strategies, goals, and distinctive features.
- ❦ **Analyze the competition.** Dig deep to understand the strategies of the competition and what makes them successful.
- ❦ **Link the specific work that the team does to the organization's strategy.** Devour information about the company, its financials, industry trends, and global trends.
- ❦ **Become students of strategy and continue development.** Seek input from those in the organization who are perceived by others to have a broad strategic vision.

There are a variety of methods to gather information that will assist in formulating a vision. Utilizing surveys to determine needs of customers and clients is a good first step. Benchmarking with similar organizations and analyzing the competition is essential. It's important to analyze data in your specific field to uncover practices that could lead to improvements in your department.

Miguel and the physician leaders on his team created a survey for patients and their families to determine what was needed to improve their experiences. They analyzed data in their specialty to understand what was being done elsewhere and how those practices elevate their department's performance. Being researchers, Miguel and the team devoured not only the research and clinical data, but also financial and trend information.

Compose a Strategic Vision Statement

A strategic vision will become an inspirational vision for the department, team, or organization. It will paint a picture of the organization, and its dreams and hopes for the future. It will serve as inspiration and a touchstone for moving forward. It should be ambitious, future-oriented, and describe activities planned for upcoming years, reaching beyond current accomplishments. A strategic vision should be purpose-driven and define what the team aims to achieve, think, feel, and say about itself in the future, distinctly capturing the language that encapsulates the particular industry or specialty. A strategic vision statement should be short, believable, and achievable.

Some examples of strategic vision statements include the following:

- **Alzheimer's Association**—A world without Alzheimer's disease
- **Teach for America**—One day, all children in this nation will have the opportunity to attain an excellent education
- **Southwest Air**—To become the world's most loved, most flown, and most profitable airline
- **Nike**—Bring inspiration and innovation to every athlete in the world

As the process of developing the team's strategic vision unfolds, in-depth conversations are in order. The team should discuss how far the department has come, how big it has grown (when applicable), where it has excelled, who it has served, and what needs to improve so they can perform and serve at the highest levels.

Miguel's team became excited by his vision and brought their own ideas, insights, and creativity to the discussions. Their enthusiasm was bolstered by Miguel's confidence in them, through the information they had gathered, and by their accomplishments to date. As the discussions ensued, they agreed that to achieve a vision of growth for the future, they would need to do the following:

- Earn recognition as best-in-class physicians
- Apply for and win increased funding
- Lead their field in cutting-edge research
- Produce a large quantity of high quality, peer-reviewed publications
- Build relationships with strategic partners
- Increase the number and types of surgeries and procedures they perform

After many discussions and iterations, Miguel and his team decided upon this strategic vision statement:

> *We will transform our surgical specialty in healing through advancements fueled by innovation and groundbreaking research.*

The team members agreed that this statement encompassed the important aspects of where they had been, where the department was currently, how the field was advancing, and where they wanted to be in the future. As the physicians and other team members clarified the elements needed to achieve their vision, they strengthened their relationships with one another and became eager to grow the department. Each committed to working toward the vision together as a team, utilizing the contributions of each team member in a unified whole.

Formulate a Workable Action Plan

The final step in developing a strategic vision is a practical plan that includes these elements:

- **Goals.** Goals include targets for increased revenue, partnerships, geographic reach, and research for the next two to three years.
- **Action steps.** Each goal includes the action steps for what team members need to do and include clearly defined action steps.
- **Clearly delineated responsible parties.** Each action step clearly states who is responsible for achieving it. Accountability is essential to success.
- **Timelines and due dates.** It is clear when all action steps are expected to be completed. These milestones are an essential element in ensuring action steps are completed.
- **Adapt as needed.** Flexibility in the face of changing circumstances is built in, because strategic visions have many moving parts and intersecting responsibilities. Mechanisms for getting intelligence and data in real time are integrated so that the team can respond to the changing environment.

Miguel and his team developed specific goals for each aspect of the vision. He worked to engage his department physicians in understanding the need for their involvement and, in so doing, he assured there were specific activities related to the goals. His management team members understood and documented their roles in achieving certain tasks and in supporting the physicians in theirs. Timelines and due dates became clear once the goals, action steps, and responsible parties were decided and assigned. Miguel assured communication mechanisms were in place to keep his entire team informed of progress and next steps.

Chapter Six—Your Best Team, includes more information on strategic action plans and how they contribute to team effectiveness. But first, let's start Cooking It Up with an opportunity to apply the content of this chapter to you and your team.

——— COOKING IT UP: RECIPE FOR YOUR VISION! ———

Mise en Place: Your Mindset for Vision

The first critical step in creating a vision is getting into the right frame of mind. Contemplating a vision is not easy when going from one task to another. It requires thought and reflection. Set some time aside, preferably in a spot you enjoy (perhaps a garden or a quiet room), and take some deep breaths.

A great way to get in this frame of mind is to answer the Miracle Question:

> *How would things be if you woke up one morning, five years from now, and you were living the professional life you wanted to live?*

Imagine your work is flowing and the vision you have had for your work as a leader is being fulfilled. Your team is functioning at the highest level possible, charting new ground, creating new models, and bringing in revenue from a variety of sources.

- ❦ What are you doing?
- ❦ What do others see you doing?
- ❦ How do others know the "miracle" has occurred without you telling them?

Jot down a few images.

Step #1: Define Your Personal Vision

Consider these questions from page 15 and write the answers on a separate piece of paper:

- ❦ When have I been happiest in the past, and what elements of that time can I take into the future?
- ❦ What am I doing now that would bring me more fulfillment if I could do it even more successfully?
- ❦ What strengths of mine fuel my vision?
- ❦ What is the highest level at which I can contribute?
- ❦ What gap am I uniquely qualified to close?
- ❦ How will I bring these talents and gifts to my role?

Step #2: Write Your Personal Vision Statement

Based on Step #1 and what you know, describe your vision of five years from now, using this template:

Five years from now, I will be successfully _____, using some of the talents and strengths that got me to where I am today, including _____, _____, and _____. I will build on what I have done so far by contributing even more in the following ways: _____.

Step #3: Develop a Strategic Vision with Your Team

You are now on your way to helping clarify a strategic vision for yourself, your team, and your department. Use the following template to help you plan the meetings you will have with your team to develop your strategic vision. Note the date you plan to convene the team for the first meeting.

STRATEGIC VISION PROCESS—LEADERSHIP STEPS

My vision is to :

Description	Elements	What You Will Say
Introduce the Process		
• Meet one-to-one with key influencers on the team • Announce at team meetings	• Convey your personal vision • Get agreement on working together as a team	
Clarify the Mission		
• Lead discussions to articulate what they are doing currently as the foundation for the future.	• Attainable • Clear • Credible • Inspiring • Unique	
Describe How Your Team Will Strategically Gather Essential Information		
• Define internal and external factors critical to formulating and reaching the vision	• Competition • Customers and client input • Organization's strategy • Students of strategy • SWOT: Review current state	
Describe What Is Included in the Strategic Vision Statement		
• Statement that will serve as a beacon going forward for the team. • Vision encompasses the elements necessary for success	• Inspiring and challenging • Future oriented: purpose-driven • Distinct and unique • Short, believable, and achievable • Discuss and identify key elements of the strategic vision	
Compose Your Team's Inspiring Strategic Vision Statement		
(to be completed by team!)		
Set Time in Team Meetings to Integrate the Strategic Vision into a Workable Plan		
• Goals • Action steps • Clearly delineated responsible parties • Timelines and due dates • Adapt as needed		

Add Your Secret Sauce

Think about the unique interests and experience you bring to your leadership of this team that can add energy and "zest" to your vision. What are some things you enjoy that you can integrate into this vision? Maybe you love history and can bring examples of successes from the past or even take the team on a field trip to an historic site that brings relevance. Bringing in your interest in sports, the arts, food, or hobbies will fuel your energy and make your vision unique to you. Describe how you'll use your secret sauce to spice up your vision.

Tastings—Tidbits for Your Team

Engage your team in the exciting process of developing a guiding vision. I'll continue to discuss working with teams in Chapter 4—The Right Cookware. For now, here are some ways you can get the team involved and excited about your vision for the future:

- Encourage your team members to complete the exercises in Cooking It Up and develop their own personal vision statements.
- Open team meetings by having team members take turns sharing their own vision and how it supports the success of the team.
- Provide copies of a book on strategic skills and agree to discuss the chapters together in a team book club.
- Schedule time to work through the strategic visioning process described in this chapter.
- Then celebrate the team's vision!

Strengths...
Your Magic Ingredient

When do you soar as a leader? What sets you apart from everyone else? What part of being a leader do you love? The answer to each of these questions is a clue pointing to one or more of your strengths. Knowing and using your strengths well is one of most important steps you can take to ensure your and your organization's success. Plus, it's a lot more fun than focusing on your weaknesses!

Think about a chef you know. It might be someone you know personally or a celebrity chef such as Giada De Laurentiis or Emeril Lagasse. That chef's identity and reputation is based on his or her unique combination of skill, experience, and interest. The best chefs know that since they can't be good at everything, they are most successful when they focus on that at which they are the best. The best burgers, the best Thai, the best seafood, presented beautifully, and delivered with the right amount of flair—fantastic!

When we were children growing up and learning, an emphasis on achieving mastery across many subjects was necessary to prepare us to succeed in the world. Most of us grew up in cultures where emphasis was put more on what we needed to do better rather than on what we already did well. No matter how many "A's" were on the report card, the "B" and lower grades got the attention. Unfortunately, when we carry this need for mastery into adulthood, we consistently focus more on our weaknesses than our strengths. As adults, this actually hurts our abilities to expand our skills and capabilities.

According to Marcus Buckingham and Ashley Goodall in their book *Nine Lies About Work*, "A strength . . . is an activity that makes you feel strong." These authors go on to say that before you do something at which you are strong, you will find yourself looking forward to it. While you're performing that activity or task, you lose track of time. In fact, time seems to pick up speed. And after you've completed the activity, you feel lifted up and proud. In other words: you experience positive anticipation beforehand, flow during, and fulfillment afterward. This combination is how you identify a strength, and results in a yearning to keep performing the activity.

A shift in emphasis from weakness to strength is important and is often profound. The Gallup organization conducted a 40-year study of human strengths that ignited a global conversation on the topic. Based on the work of scientists led by Donald O. Clifton, a pioneer in strengths psychology, a language of thirty-four basic strengths was created. This led to the creation of the CliftonStrengths assessment.

To date, millions of people from around the world have taken this assessment. In recent years, while continuing to learn even more about strengths, Gallup scientists have also been examining decades of data on the topic of leadership. They studied more than one million work teams, conducted more than 20,000 in-depth interviews with leaders, and interviewed over 10,000 followers around the world to ascertain the significance of focusing upon strengths in regard to productivity, engagement at work, and effective leadership.

In *Strengths Based Leadership*, author Tom Rath and leadership consultant Barry Conchie reveal the results of this research, including three keys to being a more effective leader:

❦ Knowing your strengths and investing in others' strengths
❦ Getting people with the right strengths on your team
❦ Understanding and meeting the four basic needs team members have for leadership: trust, compassion, stability, and hope

This research conclusively reveals that you'll get more "bang for your buck" if you focus predominantly on your own and others' strengths, rather than on weaknesses. This is the most effective way to help yourself and your team members expand capacity. Do you need to address your weaknesses? Certainly. But if you focus more on what you do well—naturally and through finely-honed practice—you'll have more energy to accomplish your goals and you'll enjoy the steps along the way a lot more. No one is perfect, and, as I have noted, many competencies are required for excellent leadership. The key is understanding and using the leadership strengths that you are best at and that come the easiest.

BENEFITS OF SHIFTING TO A STRENGTHS BASED PERSPECTIVE

This chapter is about shifting from concentrating on your weaknesses to fully knowing and embracing your strengths, and figuring out how to use them more often. It's also about bringing out and developing strengths in others. Here's why:

Zeroing in on Your Strengths Is Energizing

When you are utilizing your strengths, it feels like you are cruising along in fifth gear. You feel a sense of confidence and calm. Energy is created, in part, because you are operating efficiently. With that energy, you are also able to be innovative: solve problems, identify opportunities, and create the new. How exciting is that!

Knowing Your Unique Combination of Strengths Reveals Your Secret Sauce

According to the Gallup organization, there is a 1 in 33 million chance that you have the same combination of strengths as someone else. Others have strengths similar to yours, but they don't have the combination of strengths, talents, and life experiences that make you unique. Just as two chefs who specialize in the same type of cuisine create different dining experiences because of each chef's background, experience, and way of looking at the world, your combination of strengths and experiences combine to deliver your most powerful brand of leadership.

Articulating and Leading from Your Strengths Inspires Your Team Members

Leaders can increase their effectiveness by "announcing themselves." Using strengths language to describe to others the best way you work helps them understand how best they can work with you. Using words like analytical, futuristic, strategic, empowering, disciplined, and empathic let others know your strengths. This provides clarity, and people quickly begin to understand how best to collaborate with you. As a leader, articulating and leading from your strengths is great modeling, and it helps build a strong and cohesive team.

Leading on the Basis of Strengths Increases Productivity

A comprehensive study by Gallup on the effects of focusing on strengths revealed positive results in the following areas:

- ❦ 10-19 percent increase in sales
- ❦ 14-29 percent increase in profit
- ❦ 3-7 percent increase in employee engagement
- ❦ 22-59 percent decrease in safety incidents
- ❦ 6-16 point decrease in turnover in low-turnover organizations
- ❦ 26-72 point decrease in turnover in high-turnover organizations

Knowing and using your own strengths and creating a culture in which staff are encouraged to know and use theirs as well clearly leads to higher productivity, increased engagement, and higher retention.

Armani Ghrissi's Secret Sauce: Spicing Things Up

Armani Ghrissi is the sales director for an Italian food company that imports high-end products from Italy, Portugal, and Spain. Armani, who was born in Morocco and educated in England where he studied finance, came to the US in 2002, where he spent unhappy years in the banking industry. Eventually, Ghrissi realized that his strengths were a best fit in sales, coupled with his passion, which is food. His dream is to open a Moroccan restaurant one day.

Ghrissi says,

I am from Morocco, where it's a tradition for a child to spend many hours in the kitchen with the women. Growing up, I was always watching what my mom, grandmother, and three aunts were doing. At about the age of five, I started helping, chopping this and that, asking questions, getting involved, and learning more about the food.

Cooking Moroccan food is an elaborate task. After eating breakfast, my mom, grandmother, and aunts would spend three hours preparing lunch. I've always been amazed how these people can spend so much time cooking and come up with multiple marvelous dishes. For example, in my family, you don't get one appetizer—you get four or five.

I've always found solace in a kitchen, asking questions, getting involved, learning more and more about the food business. This has served me immensely well. When I went to boarding school in London, I already knew how to cook and I made dishes for myself. To this day, I always cook my breakfast, lunch, and perhaps dinner—if not, I skip dinner. I'm a big foodie! I'm baffled at people who don't want to put much effort into cooking. My girlfriend says, "Well, some people are not like you. It's in your blood, it's in your DNA."

The thing that sets me apart and makes me unique is my love of spices. My cabinet contains over one hundred spices. I randomly buy unfamiliar spices and work with them. I like to put oil in a pan, warm it up just a little, and add the spices to simmer with the oil at a very low temperature. That is what sets my cooking apart. I can also cook a dish and put it on the table without tasting it, feeling confident that people are going to enjoy it. This is not a secret; it's more of an innate ability, a natural strength.

When I left the bank, which was not a fit for me and my strengths, I had a bit of a crisis. My girlfriend said, "Why don't you do something with food? It comes natural to you." She was right. Food is something I can always count on.

Armani's favorite spices:
- Cumin
- Zaatar
- Ras el hanout
- Saffron
- Paprika

COMPONENTS OF STRENGTHS BASED LEADERSHIP

Leadership development experts use different terms to talk about strengths. I categorize them in three categories: innate strengths, manifested strengths, and leadership competencies.

Innate Strengths

Innate strengths are capabilities that come naturally, based on a combination of genetics and environment. For example, perhaps you are always on time. Trust me, this is not one of my innate strengths. However, it is a strength of my son, Rob. From a young age, he was always ready and on time. As early as age ten, Rob spent several minutes each morning pulling together his backpack, baseball glove, lunch bag, and jacket, ultimately waiting for me by the car. Rob couldn't describe where he learned this. He surely didn't learn it from me. He just always knew the steps needed to be organized and on time. For Rob, this is an innate strength.

Fortunately, I also have my own strengths that have felt natural to me ever since I can remember. I have always collected a lot of information—books and articles (and even recipes!)—and somehow known how to categorize and synthesize them. I am able to bring previously unrelated resources, concepts, and ideas together, organizing them all into a digestible whole. In the Gallup Strengths Finder language, this is called the "input" strength. I use this input strength in my personal and professional life by introducing people from various parts of my life, integrating information and concepts from the wider world into my coaching conversations, even figuring out how the heck I am going to make a meal from that wide array of disparate items in the refrigerator.

One way to recognize your innate strengths is to consider when you are operating on all cylinders or in fifth gear, in a moment of flow when things come easily and you accomplish a lot. What skills and elements of your personality are you using? These are your innate strengths. Once you have identified and built your actions on these elements, you will be expressing your best self. The goal is to identify your personal combination of strengths, determine how to explain them to others, and use them more often and more effectively in your role as a leader.

Manifested Strengths

I think of manifested strengths as innate strengths that have been honed through experience, practice, and attention. Innate strengths are the raw ingredients, and manifested strengths are the fully baked bread. Innate strengths become manifested through education, skill development, and practical learning—in jobs, projects, and experience. For example, attention to detail may be an innate strength that has become manifested through application to math or science, or in another field, such as editing. An innate talent in establishing a quick rapport with people may become manifested through application in fields such as teaching or sales.

Manifested strengths are recognized through mechanisms that note achievements, including grades at school, performance reviews at work, and standardized assessments. Assessments frequently used in organizations include the DISC model, Myers-Briggs Type Indicator, and CliftonStrengths assessment (the Gallup instrument). Advantages of using these assessments include standard definitions of strengths, shared terminology, and ease in talking about strengths with coworkers and team members.

The CliftonStrengths assessment provides a list of thirty-four core strengths that are organized in into four domains, as seen on the chart on the following page. The four domains are Strategic Thinking, Executing, Influencing, and Relationship Building. In addition to being helpful in identifying strengths and providing a language for articulating these strengths, a chart like this is useful in recognizing the constellation of strengths in a team.

Definitions of these strengths can be found on the Gallup website: www.gallup.com and in the books *StrengthsFinder 2.0* and *Strengths Based Leadership*. (Note: The Cooking It Up section later in this chapter provides information on how to use the CliftonStrengths assessment and exercises to assist you in identifying and articulating your specific combination of strengths.)

Look at the following chart and note the strengths that you think you may have. Think of a few examples of how you have used these strengths. This is a great start to identifying your strengths and thinking about how you can use them more often.

IDENTIFYING STRENGTHS			
Strategic Thinking	Executing	Influencing	Relationship Building
• Analytical • Contextual (thinking about the past) • Futuristic • Ideation (fascinated by ideas) • Input (like to collect and archive—like me!) • Intellection • Learner • Strategic	• Achiever • Arranger • Belief (unwavering core values) • Consistency • Deliberative • Discipline • Focus • Responsibility • Restorative (adept at dealing with problems)	• Activator • Command (presence) • Communication • Competition • Maximizer (make good things great) • Self-Assurance • Significance (want to make a big impact) • WOO (winning others over)	• Adaptability • Connectedness • Developer • Empathy • Harmony • Includer • Individualization • Positivity • Relator

Identifying strengths, articulating them, and encouraging executives to use them often is the core of my work as a leadership coach. Shifting from a mindset of deficiency to one of boundless opportunities using strengths is frequently transformative for my clients. It is energizing, efficient, and exciting!

Jada, a brilliant scientist with a PhD and years of experience in healthcare research, is an example of a leader who went through this transformation. After years of working in medical research, Jada was promoted to a senior leadership role in a large health system, leading a new system-wide initiative at the intersection of healthcare and technology. The initiative required Jada to build a highly visible department that would collaborate across many functions of the organization.

Jada sought leadership coaching in order to become a more effective leader. She had received feedback that at times she was not a team player, that she sometimes expected too much too soon, and that her impatience sometimes resulted in a disconnect from her peers and team members. From my first meeting with Jada, it became clear to me that her focus on what she perceived she was doing wrong prevented her from appreciating how many strengths she brought to this role. She knew she needed to better communicate with her team and manage frustration. I encouraged her to begin shifting her mindset to consider what strengths she could apply to these challenges.

Jada and I began by using an assessment tool so she could get a better understanding of herself in a leadership role. The results reminded Jada of the strengths that had gotten her to her current position, and we discussed how she could use them even more in her current role. The assessment revealed Jada's top six strengths:

Strategic Thinking:	Executing:
♣ Analytical	♣ Deliberative
♣ Strategic	♣ Discipline
♣ (An avid) Learner	♣ Focused

Jada and I discussed ways she could apply these strengths to her current situation. We analyzed her assessment results to fully understand her strengths and determine which ones to use in various situations. Using her Strategic Thinking skills of Analytical and Strategic, she devised strategies to communicate and implement the vision and the strategy of the program. She used these same strengths to set clear, attainable goals for each person in the work group.

Jada was initially concerned that none of her top six strengths were in the Relationship Building categories. We took a deep dive into the report and saw that adaptability and individualization were in her top ten strengths. Together we analyzed how she could use all of her strengths to reach her goals—to build a more effective team and increase her collaboration with her team members and peers. We strategized about how to use the strengths that come naturally to her in new and different ways.

Leadership Competencies

Innate and manifested strengths are the "how" of your leadership. The "what" of leadership are leadership competencies. These are the skills and behaviors required to lead others in the organization, manage yourself while doing it, and influence others in order to accomplish the organization's goals.

The path to translating your strengths into leadership competencies (behaviors) starts with envisioning the end and working backward. Just as a chef might imagine cooking a beautiful spinach soufflé, a leader needs to imagine what he or she wants to do (cook) and then figure out what it will take to make it happen: the ingredients, the preparations, and the sequence.

Many organizations create a list of competencies specific to their leadership needs. The most common leadership competencies include the categories of leading self, leading others, and leading the organization as shown below.

Leading Self

✤ Demonstrating ethics and integrity

✤ Displaying drive and purpose

✤ Exhibiting leadership stature

✤ Increasing your capacity to learn

✤ Managing yourself

✤ Increasing self-awareness

✤ Developing adaptability

Leading Others

✤ Building and maintaining relationships

✤ Communicating effectively

✤ Developing others

✤ Managing effective teams and work groups

✤ Valuing diversity and difference

Leading the Organization

✤ Managing change

✤ Managing politics and influencing others

✤ Taking risks and innovating

✤ Setting vision and strategy

✤ Managing the work

✤ Enhancing business skills and knowledge

✤ Understanding and navigating the organization

You may be thinking, "How can I possibly be good at all of these competencies?" That is the million-dollar question! No one can! The secret lies in knowing yourself, your strengths, and how you can best use these strengths to lead others and encourage them to follow you. Some will come easily, and you should think about those as being the basis of your leadership strengths moving forward. Perhaps you are really strong in communicating and recognizing the talents in others. Put your focus there. You may need to become more proficient in select competencies that really matter in your role—perhaps managing change or understanding and navigating the organization. But you may never excel at these as you would in other areas. As I say to my coaching clients, maybe you just need to get from a four to a six on a ten-point scale. The trick is to identify the most important competencies needed to be effective in your role and, if needed, focus on building one to two competencies at a time.

Jada recognized that she needed to strengthen her skills in several competencies to be most effective in her role. She came to see how important it is to be self-aware and manage frustration, particularly with staff who were not working with diligence. She continually worked on building her skills in communication and managing the teams effectively. Jada realized that while she communicated effectively in some ways, she needed to focus on communicating goals and expectations clearly.

INTEGRATING STRENGTHS INTO LEADERSHIP

There are countless ways to lead and effectively use innate and manifested strengths in leadership competencies. The following model shows how strengths and competencies combine to create a whole.

Once again, the key is to know yourself—what you do well, what you can do more often—and effectively and efficiently apply those skills to leading. Your strengths and experiences are personal to you, so how you display these competencies will be reflected in that unique combination. Because there are countless ways to display leadership responsibilities, it is important to find your own way of doing them, the one that is the most efficient and satisfying.

As you work to build and display your leadership competencies, align your efforts with your vision and goals. Depending upon your role and where you want to go, some competencies will be more important than others. For example, you may be in an organization where managing change may be essential right now because of the industry demands. It's all about knowing what is essential and when.

Another important skill is knowing how to utilize complementary staff. Since you can't be great at every competency, you need to identify who you need around you to assist in accomplishing your leadership responsibilities.

COOKING IT UP: RECIPE FOR USING YOUR STRENGTHS!

You now have the opportunity to pull all of this information together and clarify your great combination of strengths that you can use often in your leadership. Here we go!

Mise en Place—Developing a Strengths Based Mindset

Developing a mindset that focuses on your strengths rather than your weaknesses requires a shift in thinking about where to put your focus in your own development, as well as in the development of your team members. This may initially be a bit uncomfortable, since many of us are so accustomed to focusing on improving our weaknesses.

Set aside time to reflect about how you think about yourself and your strengths, talents, and weaknesses.

❦ How well do you take compliments?
❦ How often do you think about your strengths?
❦ Do you concentrate only on your negative traits and things you need to do better?

♣ How do you think about yourself as a leader:
- Are you "pretty good?"
- Are you "great" at some things?

Leading from your strengths starts with focusing more on what you are good at and what you love doing. This shift takes practice! So, make a commitment to start focusing on where you excel, and when you find yourself thinking about a weakness, consciously shift your focus to a strength.

Step #1: Identify Your Innate Strengths

Reflect on the strengths you have used ever since you can remember, the ones that come naturally. Make a list of personal characteristics that define you in a positive way by answering these questions:

♣ What have you always enjoyed doing? What comes easily to you?
♣ What have you been like when participating in teams? Competitive? Team player? Team leader? Jokester?
♣ When are you in fifth gear, soaring along, feeling your best?
♣ Think of your best subjects in school. What strengths did you bring that helped you excel?
♣ When have people consistently complimented you for doing something well?

Step #2: Identify Your Manifested Strengths Using an Assessment

Here are two options:

♣ **Option A**—Review the results of assessment tools you have taken in the past two years, e.g., DISC, Myers-Briggs, etc.
♣ **Option B**—Take a standardized assessment tool. I suggest the CliftonStrengths assessment. It's easy to access and simple to take. You can choose one of two easy ways to access the assessment:
- Go to www.gallup.com, sign up, and take the assessment. There are several different levels and corresponding prices—the most basic is fine.

- Buy a book: *StrengthsFinder 2.0* or *Strengths Based Leadership*. An access code is provided at the back of each book, which you can use on their website to take the assessment. The advantage of the books is that there is great information in each of them and the cost of the assessment is included in the price of the book.

Step #3: Develop a Strengths Plan

After you have taken the strengths assessment, it's time to identify and clarify your strengths so you can be deliberate about using them, draw upon them more often, and explain yourself to others. Review your report and reflect upon it.

- ♣ From your perspective, how accurate is the report?
- ♣ What did you already know about yourself that was confirmed?
- ♣ What surprised you about your top five strengths?
- ♣ Note the developmental suggestions that are most applicable to you.
- ♣ Note your most important strengths below, along with developmental suggestions from the assessment, and how you'll use these strengths more often.

MY STRENGTHS PLAN		
My Top Strengths (Innate and Manifested)	Developmental Suggestion	One Way I Can Use This More Often

Note, it can be very helpful to review your list of strengths with someone you trust. Get their input on this list and ask for feedback on how you can use your strengths more often.

Add Your Secret Sauce

Your secret sauce is what you bring to your life and work that helps set you apart. So do your strengths. When combined, your secret sauce is a "strengths multiplier!" It's like adding spice to the dish—only in the form of interest, energy, and vitality. How do you spend time outside of work and what strengths do you display there? Think about your interests and how you can integrate them into your work. Gardening? Bring in more plants to the office. Love the theater? Plan an outing with your team to a local production. Interested in contemporary art? Decorate your walls! Remember, as my mother used to say, "There is only one **you** in the world." Bring it on!

Tastings—Tidbits for Your Team

You can have a great impact on your team by talking more about their strengths and focusing on ways they can use them more often. Here are some suggestions:

- ☙ **Get in the habit of talking about strengths.** Discuss with your team the ways you each already bring your strengths to the team.
- ☙ **Talk about strengths as an icebreaker at your team meetings.** Take five minutes and ask team member dyads to talk to each other about their perception of their greatest strengths and their observations of their partner's greatest strength. Have the participants report out to the team and make a list of the strengths.
- ☙ **Post the list of your greatest strengths on your wall.**
- ☙ **Consider having your team members take the CliftonStrengths assessment**. Provide them with the instructions from this chapter and have them reflect on their strengths.

Ingredient #3

Is This Too Spicy?
Feedback and Understanding Perceptions of Your Leadership

In Chapter 2, I discussed the importance of identifying and using your strengths. That shift in emphasis away from focusing on what you need to improve upon—your weaknesses—to utilizing your strengths and talents is a central theme of this book. Yet, it is also important to identify key areas for improvement, in a constructive way, and preferably on an ongoing basis. That's where feedback comes in; it's an essential element to improving your leadership effectiveness. By seeking suggestions on ways you can improve, you put yourself in a better position to grow.

Leaders increase their effectiveness when they regularly seek input from staff, peers, and superiors by answers to questions including the following:

- What do you see as my greatest strengths?
- How can I use these strengths to help you be more effective?
- What are one or two ways I can be even more effective in leading you?
- How can we, together, have a greater impact?

This sounds logical, right? Most leaders acknowledge the logic but still find feedback a scary prospect, at least to some degree. Some say what most are thinking: "I'm not sure I want to know what others think. It might be painful." Welcome to the club!

When I start the coaching process with leaders, they agree that getting feedback is a good idea—at first. As we start talking about how we will actually be soliciting that feedback, however, they inevitably get cold feet. A recent conversation I had with James is pretty typical:

James: (Nervous laughter) Whoa, I bet you find that a lot of bad stuff comes out in these feedback interviews, right?

Me: Actually, no. It's more common that the leaders I work with are deeply touched by how much people appreciate their strengths, and how they could have been using them much more often to make their job feel easier.

James: Mmmm, that's great. But what if I find out that some people don't think I am a very good leader?

Me: It's more likely that they'll point out a few blind spots, things you have ignored, or thought were not that important, but that actually get in the way of your effectiveness. We all have things about us that we know we could do better or that we have struggled with for years, but we have put them off and gotten by.

James: I think some of the feedback will be good and some not so good. I guess we'll see!

Me: That usually is the case. One of the great things about feedback is that it can increase your understanding of diverse points of view by people who know you. People have different expectations of you as a leader. For one person on your team, your leadership approach may be a bit too "spicy," while for another, it is not spicy enough. Feedback can help you increase your menu of leadership behaviors.

James: Okay. I guess there's no way to get out of this, right?

Me: Nope. It will be fine!

I coached an administrator who was constantly sending his peers in-depth articles to read about their areas of specialization, encouraging them to read them and get back to him with their thoughts. While realizing this was well intended, some found it off-putting. They would prefer he sit down and talk with them directly about how they could work together more effectively. Once the administrator realized this, he began prioritizing meetings with his peers, and as a result, respect for him as a leader increased significantly.

Receiving feedback can be a stressful experience. According to author and social scientist Joseph Grenny in the *Harvard Business Review* article "How to Be Resilient in the Face of Harsh Criticism," "We all crave approval and fear truth. And critical feedback feels traumatic because it threatens two of our most fundamental psychological needs:

safety (perceived physical, social, or material security) and worth (a sense of self-respect, self-regard, or self-confidence)." That's why many people hesitate to ask for feedback.

But the more routine feedback becomes, the less stressful it is to initiate. That is why it is so important to integrate feedback conversations regularly into the daily interactions you have with your team members, boss, and peers. Research shows that the more current the feedback, the more relevance it has and the easier it is to accept. Receiving and providing feedback regularly and frequently can reduce defensiveness; it will become part of the team culture.

Chef Smith's Secret Sauce:
Feedback Drives You to Get Better

Chef Charles "Chaz" Smith is founder of The Culinary Artist Gourmet Catering Group, as well as a multi-faceted artist and entrepreneur. He worked his way up in fine dining from garde-manger to waiter captain to general manager to executive chef. Eventually, Chef Smith opened his restaurant, Chaz & Odette, where his dishes were mentioned by Zagat as "some of Pittsburgh's best!" (2014). He ultimately launched his successful catering business, fueled by a stint co-hosting the TV show "Grill It" with Bobby Flay.

Chef Smith says:

> My maternal grandmother, Mimi, cultivated and encouraged my adventurous palate by taking me to eat at fancy restaurants. I tried escargot and foie gras between ages nine and ten. One summer, when I was eleven, she took me on a tour of the South through West Virginia, Kentucky, Tennessee, and Mississippi, where I enjoyed classics such as cornmeal fried catfish, spoonbread, red-eye gravy, and Mississippi mud pie. That trip ignited the travel bug in me,

and I've since experienced the food and culture of a dozen countries, adding new flavors to my culinary repertoire.

In my catering business, feedback, which is essential, is immediate. At a multi-cultural fraternity (of which I am a brother), I've prepared dishes from around the world, serving a buffet-style lunch and dinner five days a week for sixty hungry guys over the past eight years. I love it! I put out the food, and a host of guys line up to eat it. While we are cleaning up, they come into the kitchen with their empty plates telling me, "That was awesome, Chef!"

The immediate feedback is important, and the compliment is always appreciated. Even more, I appreciate hearing when a dish was not a big hit. That's how I improve as a chef. I'm always asking myself, "What could I have done differently to make that dining experience better than it was?" It's the pursuit of perfection that drives excellence.

Chef Chaz was featured in a recent issue of *Table Magazine*, where he shared the following recipe:

Island Brown Chicken Stew

Ingredients:

8 chicken thighs, bone-in, skin on
1 lime, wedged lengthwise
1/4 cup vegetable oil + 3 tbsp for browning
5 tbsp AP flour + more for dredging
1 yellow onion, large, 1/2-inch dice
1 large green bell pepper, 1/2-inch dice
3 celery stalks, 1/2-inch dice
2-1/2 cups hot water
1 tbsp tomato paste
1 tbsp Kitchen Bouquet (or Gravy Master)
1 tbsp garlic, minced (3 cloves)
1 tsp thyme, dried
Salt and pepper, to taste
1/2 tsp red pepper flakes (optional)

3 scallions cut hard on the bias
1 small bunch cilantro or parsley

Instructions:

Wash chicken thighs and then rub with lime wedges. Season with salt and pepper. Allow to rest 1 hour. Heat 3 tablespoons of oil in a Dutch oven on medium-high heat. Dust and dredge the chicken in flour and brown each piece on both sides. Remove and set aside. Sauté the onion, green pepper, and celery in the Dutch oven until softened, about 3 to 5 minutes. Add 5 tablespoons of flour and 1/4 cup vegetable oil to the Dutch oven, lower heat, and cook, stirring constantly until medium-light brown, about 10 minutes. Slowly add hot water, one ladle at a time, to make a thick sauce. Add tomato paste, Kitchen Bouquet, garlic, and thyme. Return chicken to the Dutch oven; reduce heat to low and cover. Simmer on stovetop or place in 350-degree oven for 90 minutes. Season to taste with salt, pepper, and red pepper flakes (if using), and serve with rice and peas or plain steamed rice with extra gravy. Garnish with sliced scallions and cilantro or parsley.

ADOPTING A GROWTH MINDSET

The ability to receive and integrate feedback is affected by the mindset the leader adopts. Psychologist Carol Dweck has contributed groundbreaking research that distinguishes between a growth mindset and a fixed mindset. Initially intrigued by how different children responded to failure to complete a puzzle set before them, Dweck noticed that some children actually embraced a difficult challenge or failure as an opportunity to learn. Sparked by that observation, Dweck spent thirty years researching people's beliefs about failure.

Dweck published a groundbreaking book called *Mindset: The New Psychology of Success* that changed the way experts talk about mental constructs regarding learning and failure. The book revealed that people establish one of two mindsets from our parents, teachers, and other authority figures in our lives. The two options are either a fixed mindset or a growth mindset. People with a fixed mindset believe, consciously or unconsciously, that the intelligence, abilities, and talents they have were present at birth. In other words, their qualities are fixed and can't be changed. This mindset creates a need to project competence and strength, while hiding any weaknesses.

Those children Dweck observed who embraced failure as a learning opportunity had a growth mindset, which is based on the belief that intelligence, abilities, and talents can be cultivated through effort, strategy, and help from others. When people with a growth mindset don't feel up to a task or challenge, they seek to get better. They may choose to do research, build a skill, ask an expert, or experiment with options. Generally speaking, they don't feel the need to hide the fact they have room for improvement. People with a growth mindset believe that the abilities they are born with are simply a starting point.

Adopting a growth mindset increases your effectiveness as a leader and can dramatically impact the way you both give and receive feedback. Demonstrating your intent to receive input and information to assist you in continual improvement sends an important message to your team: we are always learning, we can take risks, and we can adjust along the way. A growth mindset fuels the perspective that effective leadership is a journey, with opportunities to learn at every turn. Viewing this process as positive, necessary, and helpful is transformative, both for you and for those around you.

———————————————————

Stacey, a director in the department of learning and development at a large university, had an experience with feedback which demonstrates its power and how integral it can be to leadership success. Stacey was a rising star in the organization, and she thought of herself as being extremely successful. This perception was reinforced by a recent promotion. She was deadline driven and committed to doing a great job.

Following several conversations with me about a significant conflict Stacey was having with a colleague, Stacey realized that she needed help in managing conflict and working with challenging people. Stacey also admitted that when under pressure, she worked too hard, stayed up late, worried a lot, and, as a result, became irritable and demanding.

During my coaching with Stacey, we implemented a process to obtain input from a number of superiors, peers, and staff members she had identified. The feedback revealed that, in a nutshell, Stacey's behavior was driving her team nuts! She wasn't particularly good at giving them realistic deadlines; she was unable to say no to her boss; and she unrealistically loaded up the department with responsibilities that were beyond their ability to handle.

Stacey began to see how critical it was for her to examine these behaviors in her role as a leader. Some of the things that Stacey valued most about herself, characteristics and behaviors that had helped her ascend to her leadership position, were no longer as useful or effective. Her perfectionism was causing extreme stress in her team members. And her high emotionality, while at times endearing, interfered with effectiveness, particularly when she and the team were under pressure.

Stacey needed to temper her willingness to take on projects with learning to say no and risking the ire of her boss. This was a key lesson for her. She realized that she needed to engage her boss to set realistic goals with corresponding plans, provide realistic deadlines, and negotiate for resources, instead of taking it all on and overloading herself and her team.

The feedback process helped Stacey gain insight into how managing her emotions in the moment, particularly when she felt under stress, was integral to her future success. She learned habits to manage her stress and techniques to keep her emotions in check, including simple ones, such as taking deep breaths and counting to ten before responding.

Without feedback from others, Stacey would likely have continued to use the skills that got her to a position of leadership, those that were no longer as useful and contributing to conflict and stress for her and her team. Feedback provided the mechanism for Stacey to get valuable input, insight, and suggestions from others to help her keep growing and adapting. Because of her willingness to receive feedback and respond to it, Stacey was able to become a much better leader to her team and find more satisfaction in her leadership role.

Stacey's experience exemplifies the story of many leaders:

⚜ Her significant strengths and talents had propelled her into a leadership role.
⚜ Some of the strengths that served her well in the past were not as useful in her leadership role.
⚜ Getting feedback helped her see where change was needed, where building skills would have the most positive, immediate impact.

THE WHO, WHAT, WHEN, AND HOW OF FEEDBACK

Some organizations provide leadership coaches to solicit feedback for their leaders; others use online 360° tools; others expect leaders to solicit feedback according to their individual style. Whatever the method, it is important to establish the understanding that feedback is for the purpose of supporting success. It is most effective when it is timely, frequent, and specific—focusing as much as possible on specific behaviors.

How to Get Feedback

You'll want to choose a process that yields meaningful, helpful information and engages others, while being simple enough to be replicable. The process you choose will be influenced by the number of people from whom you desire feedback. Options include the following:

- One-to-one conversations with key people
- Confidential surveys from a neutral source, such as Survey Monkey
- Designated time during team meetings
- Designated time as part of performance review conversations
- Routine practice at important junctures, such as when important projects are finished or new ones are launched

Whom to Ask for Feedback

Choose a cross-section of people who have the opportunity to observe your behavior and can provide their perceptions: some superiors, direct reports, and peers. You may also choose to solicit feedback from customers, clients, and/or members of the community.

The number of people involved depends upon the method you choose to gather the feedback. For example, if the feedback is being solicited in face-to-face conversations or interviews, typically eight to ten people are included. If the information is gathered through a standardized online assessment, the pool can be significantly larger. Ideally, gather at least some of the information through a confidential mechanism.

Renowned executive coach Marshall Goldsmith wrote in *What Got You Here Won't Get You There*, "In my experience the best solicited feedback is *confidential* feedback. It's good because nobody gets embarrassed or defensive . . . You're merely ingesting honest commentary—which you requested!—from blind but well-meaning sources."

What to Ask

Goldsmith describes the feedback process as essentially discovering how a leader can improve or do better. In my coaching practice, I find that most leaders benefit by getting feedback in the competencies that are essential to leadership effectiveness: communicating clearly, managing conflict productively, building and leading effective teams, and increasing political acumen.

Here are some suggested questions. It is best to ask three or four for feedback in conversational settings. When using a survey, more can be included. The goal is to gather the most useful information on your strengths and how to use them more often, and the leadership behaviors that are most important for you to improve. (You'll have the opportunity to decide the most useful questions for you to use in the Cooking It Up section.)

- ❦ What two suggestions do you have for improving my work?
- ❦ What could I do to make your job easier?
- ❦ What can I do to communicate better?
- ❦ How could I handle my projects more effectively?
- ❦ How could I do a better job of following through on commitments to you and the team?
- ❦ What is unique about me that increases your productivity?
- ❦ How could I manage stressful or conflictual situations better?
- ❦ What do you think is my "secret sauce?" How can I use it more often?
- ❦ If you had to describe me to a new hire, what would you say?
- ❦ If I were an animal what would I be?

What to Do with Feedback

Once the feedback has been requested and provided, use the following method of integrating it so that positive change can occur:

- ❦ **Summarize the feedback.** Whatever method you've used to gather the feedback, the summary process includes identifying strengths and behaviors to use more frequently, opportunities for improvement, and a few key areas in which to make behavioral change or increase competency.

❦ **Create an action plan.** Use the feedback to change or develop your leadership practice, either by increasing use of strengths or building skills in specific competencies. The feedback is most effective when put into a written plan, detailing the actions you will take, preferably with timeframes and deadlines.

❦ **Validate the action plan.** Before finalizing the behavioral changes to make, discuss the goals and action steps with one or two trusted advisers, preferably those familiar with the organization. They can assist in identifying the most important areas of focus and in honing the action steps.

❦ **Demonstrate action and follow up**. Once your action plan is finalized and you've begun implementing it, you need to convey to the key stakeholders the actions you are taking. This can be done in individual conversations, in an email, or in team meetings. Informing others of the desired change and the steps you are taking reinforces a culture of learning and mutual support for growth.

CREATING A FEEDBACK CULTURE

All great artists, athletes, writers, and researchers go through peer review to improve their contributions. Adopting this growth and quality improvement framework is important for all teams, big or small. In short, regular give-and-take feedback is an essential element in a highly functioning team.

Feedback is about improving performance and adapting as internal and external conditions change. As you know, change is constant in all areas: your own growth and experience, the demands of the role, the organization, the profession, and the economic environment.

Letting your team know that you genuinely want to receive and give feedback and talking about it, referencing it, and preparing others for it creates a culture of growth mindset. When leaders and team members think of themselves as constantly learning and improving, their thinking about feedback shifts. Instead of worrying about doing something wrong or not being good enough, the mindset shifts to one of learning and pragmatic, ongoing improvement.

Incorporate Feedback into Current Processes

As noted, feedback is most effective when it is accurate, frequent, and routine. Ways to assure that feedback becomes a normal part of the culture include the following:

❦ Build feedback into team meeting conversations.

❦ Ask for and provide feedback informally as well as through formal channels.

❦ Follow up big projects by asking for feedback on how everyone, including you, can improve.

Be a Role Model

When it comes to demonstrating the importance of feedback, the greatest motivator for others is to show them their feedback is appreciated, considered, and applied, as appropriate. You can bet that once employees have taken the time to give their opinion on a matter, they'll watch to see if their opinion is truly valued. It's also important to listen for feedback, however it comes to you. Paying attention to ongoing feedback, even when given casually, sets the expectation that feedback is a normal part of doing business.

Set Ground Rules About Feedback

Established guidelines for feedback help team members to feel comfortable and safe with both giving and receiving feedback.

❦ Communicate the belief that feedback is for the purpose of learning.

❦ Assure team members that the feedback process is separate from formal evaluation processes and will not be used for performance review.

❦ Assume the person giving feedback has good intentions.

❦ Remind team members that feedback is for calm and rational times—not during the heat of an angry or emotional moment.

❦ Remind team members that good feedback is constructive, never blaming or shaming.

When receiving feedback, remind your team members to listen deeply, get more information by asking clarifying questions, and take time to reflect on what they've heard. It's also important for them to graciously accept suggestions and say thank you!

Mentally Prepare to Give Feedback

When giving feedback yourself, be in a positive frame of mind and remember that feedback is a positive tool for improving performance. Researcher and renowned leadership expert Brené Brown suggests that leaders be able to say the following before giving feedback:

- ❦ I'm ready to acknowledge what you do well instead of picking apart your mistakes.
- ❦ I recognize your strengths and how you can use them to address your challenges.
- ❦ I can talk about how resolving these challenges will lead to growth and opportunity.

Asking for feedback, showing that you have heard and appreciated it, and demonstrating concrete changes in behavior shows your team that you are serious about learning and becoming an even more effective leader. It also sets a great example and can help reduce the worry and defensiveness that staff members often feel initially about feedback.

────── COOKING IT UP: RECIPE FOR FEEDBACK! ──────

Mise en Place—Adopting A Growth Mindset

Accepting feedback as an essential part of learning and becoming even more effective is an element of a growth mindset. Consider how you feel about receiving feedback. Do you see it as potentially threatening or helpful? Somewhere in between? Reflect on the following:

Describe a time you received positive feedback that propelled you to become even better.

- ❦ How did you react?
- ❦ What were the conditions that helped you hear and incorporate this feedback?
- ❦ What made the feedback memorable?

Describe a time you received feedback that was a negative and unhelpful experience.

- ❦ How did you react?
- ❦ What were the conditions that made the feedback unhelpful?
- ❦ How could it have been delivered more effectively?

Continue to be aware of your own experiences with receiving feedback and how they have impacted the way you receive and provide feedback.

Step #1: Design Your Feedback Process

MY FEEDBACK PROCESS

HOW: I will request feedback using these methods

Decide how you'll request the feedback.

- One-to-one conversations with key people
- A confidential survey from a neutral source, e.g., Survey Monkey
- During team meetings
- As part of performance review conversations
- At important junctures, e.g., as important projects are finished or a new one is launched

WHO: This is whom I will ask for feedback

Decide how you will assure you receive a cross-section of information and input on perceptions of your leadership. Remember that it is helpful to get feedback from superiors, peers, staff, and when applicable, customers or clients. Who are your feedback "key stakeholders?"

WHAT: This is what I will ask

Decide what you will ask. Here are some suggested questions:

- What two suggestions do you have for improving my work?
- What could I do to make your job easier?
- What can I do to communicate better?
- How could I handle my projects more effectively?
- How could I do a better job of following through on commitments to you and the team?
- What is unique about me that increases your productivity?
- How could I manage stressful or conflictual situations better?
- What do you think is my "secret sauce?" How can I use it more often?
- If you had to describe me to a new hire, what would you say?

Remember to add a question or two related specifically to the competencies that you think you need to develop.

Step #2: Summarize Your Feedback

Use the following chart to summarize your key learnings from the feedback. Note your most important strengths, along with the feedback you received, including some direct quotes when possible. Consider the following questions:

❦ What strengths did people mention that particularly moved you?

❦ How can you use those strengths more often?

❦ What steps will you take with this knowledge?

❦ What are the opportunities people mentioned that are most promising to you?

❦ What can you improve upon that will quickly escalate your leadership effectiveness?

❦ What sticks with you?

❦ What steps will you take to build this skill or competency?

Be sure to use the space allotted to capture the feedback about your secret sauce!

FEEDBACK SUMMARY		
	Feedback I Received (Description or Quotes)	What I Will Do/ Steps I Will Take
Strengths That Others See in Me		
Key Opportunities For Me To Develop		
Ways I Can Use My Secret Sauce		

Step #3: Give Feedback

MY FEEDBACK PROCESS: GIVING FEEDBACK

HOW: I will provide feedback to my direct reports using these methods

Decide how you'll provide the feedback.

- One-to-one conversations with direct reports
- During team meetings
- As part of performance review conversations
- At important junctures, e.g., as important projects are finished or a new one is launched
- A formal 360° process, using a standardized tool or interviews

WHO: This is to whom I will provide feedback

List your direct reports/team members here to whom you will provide feedback on a regular basis:

WHAT: This is the type of feedback I will provide

Here are some suggestions:

- I like the way you handled that responsibility in these specific ways.
- Here are two suggestions I have to help you be even more effective.
- Here are some suggestions for how you could handle projects more effectively.
- Here are some suggestions on how you could manage stressful or conflictual situations better.
- What is your "secret sauce?" How can you use it more often?
- What can I do to make your job easier?
- What can we do to communicate better about your responsibilities?

Remember to add comments specific to the competencies that you think this person need to develop.

Add Your Secret Sauce

Remember to request information about the parts of yourself that set you apart as you request and provide feedback to others. Sprinkle the conversation with stories and metaphors about what is interesting to you and ask your team members to do the same. Sharing stories and metaphors is a quick way to reduce tension and have an interesting conversation!

Tastings—Tidbits for Your Team

Setting a climate for development through feedback, fueled by a growth mindset, is an important step in assisting your team in continual growth and learning. Here are some steps to keep that process going:

- **Talk regularly about the importance of feedback with your team.** Remind them of your desire to receive feedback from them, and how your feedback to them and from others will help them grow.
- **Discuss tips on effective feedback:**
  - Focus more on what people are doing right, and how they can use their strengths more often.
  - Be clear about what you want to say before you say it.
  - Focus on the behavior and not the person.
  - Share your feedback in a concise and specific manner. Avoid generalizations.
  - Be descriptive rather than evaluative.
- **Encourage each team member to design his or her own feedback process**, using the template in this chapter's Cooking It Up section.
- **Encourage a growth mindset about feedback itself**. Ask team members to suggest books, articles, TED Talks, and blogs.

Ingredient #4

Sous Chef to Executive Chef …
Your Transition from Doer to Leader

A lex was a leader with an urgent need to get things done. He had just been promoted to director of communications and marketing in a mid-size healthcare technology firm. The company had grown exponentially in the past several years, and Alex's responsibilities had grown right along with the company. When we began our coaching relationship, he was drowning—working twelve- to fourteen-hour days and many weekends. He was stressed, having trouble sleeping, and grabbing food on the run.

Alex's boss was concerned about Alex's stress level and observed that Alex was not utilizing his team members as effectively as he could. Even with additional staff, key deliverables considered vital to the company's sales goals were not being met. The vice president of sales was getting restless. And no matter how hard Alex paddled, he was still swimming upstream.

Alex and I began addressing his challenges by discussing his priorities and most important responsibilities as a middle-level manager. Alex rattled off the projects he was working on: updating the website, developing conference presentations, and increasing the company's presence on social media. Alex was frustrated by constant interruptions by his team members, who kept asking him questions, requesting things from him, and expecting him to intervene in problem-solving. He described his work as jumping from one important thing to another.

I reminded him of a truth that never fails to stop a new leader in his or her tracks: his fundamental responsibility was to develop others. The color drained from Alex's face, and he looked at me as though I had three heads. "How am I going to find time for *that*? You are kidding, right?" he asked incredulously. I held my ground as we continued to talk about the need to expand capacity.

Alex was at an important transition, one which all leaders go through. This transition, from doer to a leader who focuses on getting the work done through others, is one of the most important, and challenging, changes a leader can make. This shift becomes increasingly vital to success as the leader takes on increased responsibility.

The transition from doer to leader requires changes in habits, behaviors, priorities, and skills. It requires letting go of some of the very identity that resulted in the promotion to leadership, and as the leadership role develops, spending less time using skills the leader was proficient in as an individual contributor.

Alex admitted he felt some stress and anxiety about his leadership competence, as do many leaders during this transition. At times he was grateful to "get back to the work," where he was confident about what he was doing. But Alex also knew that in order to be successful in leading his team, he was going to need to hand off much more of the work to others.

Alex began the major transition to leader, shifting his attention to developing others, so that the work could get done, the capacity could be expanded to take on more, and people could grow to be even more valuable to the organization.

Chef Branduzzi's Secret Sauce:
Remaining Calm

At twenty-two years old and fresh out of college, Chef Domenic Branduzzi opened Piccolo Forno in the Lawrenceville section of Pittsburgh, Pennsylvania. Although he is not formally trained in cooking, Chef Branduzzi grew up and worked in the kitchen at his family's bakery. There, he got a taste of cooking and serving customers.

Shortly after the passing of his father, Antonio, and the closing of the bakery in 2008, Branduzzi's mother, Carla, joined him in the kitchen at Piccolo Forno. The two work together to recreate traditional Tuscan dishes, always keeping Antonio's words in mind: "Fare Tutto con Amore," "Make everything with love."

Chef Branduzzi says,

You can have an idea of how you want things to go in your world, but really, it's a matter of taking things day by day. In the restaurant business, you never know what's going to happen. For example, things break, or multiple people fail to show up for work. Something is thrown at you every day, and it's just a matter of how you respond. You just have to figure out how to keep the restaurant going. It falls on you, the leader, to make sure that that happens.

You have to remain calm through difficult situations. You have to be able to think relationally and be willing to ask for help so the burden doesn't fall on you all the time. Fortunately, I've always been a calm individual. I got that from my father.

You have to remember that members of your team— the employees and manager with whom you surround yourself—are there to help you. The best thing to do is to come together, look at the problem, and figure out how to solve it as a team. Ultimately, we want to keep doing what we're doing, feeding people and providing a pleasurable dining experience.

I tell potential chefs the same thing my mother told me when I told her that I was going to pursue this business. She said, "If you're going to do this, you have to put your whole heart into it. When you find that you can't do that anymore, stop." She was right. If you're really passionate about the food business, you should go for it. But it's not easy. You have to put in the time, the effort, and the heart.

The pandemic gave me time to look at the food industry as a whole, including the future of restaurants and dining out. We need to accept where things are, where they are going, and how they are going to be. It will be important

> *for us to hone our take-out business, and perhaps tweak our menu to create foods that travel better. There are a lot of different moving parts in this industry, and I've used the disrupted time to reflect on my business and the restaurant business as a whole.*

EMBRACING THE SHIFT TO LEADERSHIP

In *Managing Oneself*, Peter Drucker said, "Now, most of us, even those of us with modest endowments, will have to learn to manage ourselves. We will have to learn to develop ourselves. We will have to place ourselves where we can make the greatest contribution. And we will have to stay mentally alert and engaged during a 50-year working life, which means knowing how and when to change the work we do."

The shift to prioritizing one's role as leader and the developer of others is a big one. And it can be a stressful one. A study by the international HR consulting firm Development Dimensions International (DDI) revealed that in terms of challenging experiences, getting a long-sought-after promotion is second only to dealing with a divorce. The more senior you are, the more intense the challenge. More than three quarters of the leaders DDI polled said understanding that the new role required a different way of thinking would have helped them to be more successful. All leaders rated the ability to adjust to getting work done through others as one of their top three most difficult challenges.

Jodi Detjen and Sheila Simarian Webber of Suffolk University summarized these necessary changes in their *Harvard Business Review* article "Strategic Shifts That Build Executive Leadership:"

❧ **Shift your perspective of you.** This shift is best supported by your commitment to personal and professional reflection and growth. Identify where you currently have influence, where you have the opportunity and ability to expand your control and grow your career. The process includes coming to understand the resistance you will encounter by others and how to overcome it.

❧ **Shift your perspective of others.** This requires getting input from your immediate team but not stopping there. Move beyond your immediate network and get a wider perspective of the organization from others' points of view. Ask questions, test assumptions, and learn about subject matters outside of your own area of expertise in order to identify the goals and concerns of others.

✤ **Shift responsibility.** Key to this shift is expanding the ways in which you get things done by others, which I will explore in greater depth in Chapter 5. As a skillful leader, you categorize and assign tasks, and make decisions about who is best prepared to handle those tasks and grow from the experience. This shift also involves letting go of perfection and understanding that tasks may not be done exactly the way you would do them.

✤ **Shift leverage.** You increase your leverage when you engage others across the organization in alliances and connections to look at how work and tasks can be accomplished in new and different ways.

✤ **Shift the organization.** This shift is especially exciting as it involves envisioning opportunities for the organization as a result of your expertise. You begin to see your work as a leader making positive changes in the organization. Your credibility increases, allowing you to research and network new ideas, articulate the value of your ideas, and identify needs and risks while testing out those ideas.

Making these shifts takes time, thought, and energy. As you can see from the figure on page 64, it's a multifaceted process rather than an event. It is the work of the competency category of leading self. The foundational work for leading self includes managing yourself, managing your priorities, and managing your tasks. As you explore these categories, I encourage you to think about what you already bring to this transition:

✤ What have you learned so far?

✤ What comes most easily to you?

✤ Where do your strengths shine through?

✤ How is your secret sauce an asset?

✤ What can you do to "turn up the heat" and use it more often and even more effectively?

✤ And what, if you added a new habit or a new behavior, would escalate your leadership effectiveness right now?

MANAGE YOURSELF

The shift in moving from doing tasks to overseeing others and building their capacity is a huge one, requiring a reprioritization of how you use time, focus, and energy. It requires you to change your habits and default behaviors. Managing yourself includes identifying what you can control, managing your mood, practicing mindfulness, managing your stress, and managing your energy.

Identify What You Can Control

Much of what you are responsible for is influenced and controlled by others. Outdated policies, obstinate people, inefficient processes, and short-sighted decisions made at the top can all contribute to frustration. Identifying and focusing on what you can control is a key aspect of managing yourself.

Ask yourself key questions to ascertain what is in your locus of control:

- ❧ Do I have the information, knowledge, skills, and authority to take on this situation?
- ❧ If not, what about this situation could I possibly influence?
- ❧ How will I manage my frustration about this?
- ❧ What can I do right now that will help me let this go and move onto something more productive?"

Manage Your Mood

Successful leaders are aware that their moods and emotions impact others. Your mood can set the tone for the entire team as well as for yourself and your own productivity. We all have a choice in how we respond to any situation. As a leader, you will feel negative emotions, such as fear, anger, and frustration; this is a normal part of everyone's day. But your efforts to manage those emotions—or not—have a profound impact on the morale and productivity of the group.

Eric Barker, author of the book and blog entitled *Barking Up the Wrong Tree*, which provide science-based research on living successfully, begins his list of the six things most productive people do every day with "#1: Manage Your Mood." Research in brain science reveals that positive emotions—curiosity, delight, and joy—are fleeting, like "Teflon on the brain." Conversely, humans are wired to hold onto negative emotions. Evolutionarily speaking, this makes a lot of sense; our existence as a species depended on that racing heartbeat when a predator, flood, or fire threatened, and our fight-or-flight system kicked in.

In modern life and work, this inbred reaction frequently works against us. The stressors we experience now tend to be more lasting than the fleeting ones experienced by our ancestors. We have chronic worry and anxiety about getting work done, meeting budgets, resolving difficulty with coworkers, and more. As a result, the physical reactions of our fight-or-flight response stick with us, impeding our health and performance.

Fortunately, we can engage another system known as rest-and-digest. If the gas pedal is the fight-or-flight response, the rest-and-digest system is the brakes. The fight-or-flight response is hardwired into us. We can shift to rest-and-digest, but only by consciously choosing to take action to implement the brakes. This action includes practices that allow our bodies and minds to restore and refuel.

Manage Your Stress

The first response of many people in managing their moods and stressors is to look for external fixes. They might look for a different job, hire a different employee, or move to a different geographic location. Unfortunately, these solutions are often temporary and/or ineffective. Managing stress over the long term requires cultivating resilience skills to manage the challenges and barriers that will inevitably be part of life and work. The following techniques will help you increase resilience:

❧ **Understand the root causes of your stress.** Look at the factors that are causing you stress, along with your physical and emotional responses to these factors. Determine how much you are willing, and able, to manage in your current position.

❧ **Reframe how you think about stress.** Think about stress not just as a negative, but also as a motivator. Studies show that when participants viewed their stress response as helpful it became motivating and energizing.

❧ **Link learning with action.** Seeing stressful situations as motivators and opportunities for learning and growth creates a sense of challenge and opportunity. Asking "What can I learn from this?" and keeping track of the progress you make goes a long way in utilizing stress to your advantage and building resilience for future challenges.

Manage Your Energy

Recognizing how your energy naturally fluctuates and identifying your personal prime time—your most productive time of day—is essential to your productivity. You may not have much control of what hours you are expected to be available, but you can be realistic and honest with yourself and others about when you are at your best. Schedule important projects and conversations during your peak hours, when possible, and do your best to reduce interruptions during these productive times. The following graphic offers a menu of behaviors to manage energy:

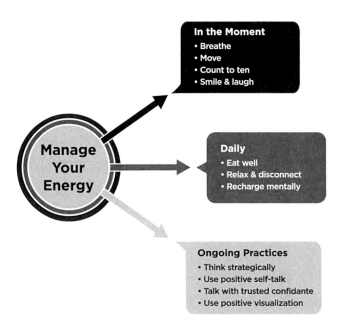

In the Moment
- Breathe
- Move
- Count to ten
- Smile & laugh

Manage Your Energy

Daily
- Eat well
- Relax & disconnect
- Recharge mentally

Ongoing Practices
- Think strategically
- Use positive self-talk
- Talk with trusted confidante
- Use positive visualization

♣ **In the moment.** Bradberry and Cleaves's book *Emotional Intelligence 2.0* has a great list of self-management strategies to stay focused in the moment. Try these strategies: take deep, cleansing breaths; get up and moving about once per hour; count to ten to break tension; and find ways to smile and laugh.

♣ **Daily.** Fuel yourself through good nutrition, drink enough water, make sure you have enough down time and relaxation, and recharge mentally.

♣ **Ongoing practices.** Build practices into your schedule that prepare you for ongoing challenges and stressful events. Allow opportunities to think strategically and solve problems, have conversations with trusted confidantes, and visualize yourself succeeding.

Practice Mindfulness

Practices such as daily meditation, yoga, quiet reflection, and journaling can positively impact not only our minds but our overall health, including lowering blood pressure and building a stronger immune system. These practices all contribute to an increased sense of well-being and better health. Practicing appreciation and engaging in a repetitive ritual of gratitude have both been proven to lead to greater well-being.

"Three Good Things" is a gratitude exercise you can build into your life as a daily habit:

♣ Every night before bed, take time to reflect back on your day.

♣ Think of three specific things that went well for you during the day.

♣ Write those three things down. Reflect on each of them.

To get the most out of this exercise, be sure to do the following:

♣ Commit to a timeline. Try this exercise every day for one week, or once a week for six weeks. Chances are you'll see results in your mood and decide to continue the practice.

♣ Write your three things down. This helps you retain the information and focus on the positive events in a structured way.

♣ Reflect on what you did to get a positive outcome. This adds to your sense of self-control and well-being.

MANAGE YOUR PRIORITIES

In these fast-paced times, it often feels as if the faucet of work is turned on and never turned off. The pressures and responsibilities of work and family can supersede the vision and the larger, longer-term goals you have for your life and work. And the balance of work and private life can feel anything but balanced! It is essential to be intentional about it, using systems that assure that your most important goals are integrated into your daily activities. The best way to reach larger goals is to break down the activities associated with them into smaller daily priorities and habits.

The Prioritization Matrix

President Dwight Eisenhower is credited with developing this widely used tool. To use the matrix, put your responsibilities or tasks in one of four categories: do, schedule, delegate, or eliminate.

PRIORITIZATION MATRIX		
	Urgent	**Not Urgent**
Important	**DO** Do it now!	**SCHEDULE** Decide a time to do it next.
Not Important	**DELEGATE** Who is best to do it?	**ELIMINATE** Delete it from consideration.

Starting each day by filling out the Prioritization Matrix is a good way to start getting a handle on your priorities and those of your team. It's tempting to just DO—and DO IT NOW! That is the trap that many fall into. The larger goals of life and work—e.g., getting big projects done, exercising regularly, strategically planning—require you to SCHEDULE, breaking down the larger goal into smaller tasks and scheduling them. Moving from prioritizing tasks that are Urgent to Not Urgent will increase your effectiveness, impact, and ultimately your satisfaction, as you learn to master the ways to get the things done that are most important to you and your organization.

Before You Try to Do It Faster, Ask Whether It Should Be Done at All

Eric Barker's research in *Barking Up the Wrong Tree* of the six things productive people do each day reveals that top-performing CEOs don't get more done by working more hours; rather, they are successful by following through on carefully executed plans. Rather than thinking of working harder, or more, think about shifting your mental energy to focus on the most important things. Go ahead and . . . say "No."

- ♱ **Say no.** This can be harder than it sounds. But it is so important in managing your priorities and making the big shift from doer to leader. It's fine to use verbal tricks to buy yourself some time, like awkwardly pausing, saying "No, but . . . ," putting the request off for a later time, saying you need to check your calendar, using humor to lighten the "no," or suggesting someone else take the lead on a project.
- ♱ **Define your goals the night before.** Take time each evening to decide the most important one or two things you want to get done the next day. Write them down.
- ♱ **Do what you love.** At the core of your prioritizing, figure out that which drives you, excites you, and makes you unique. Stay connected to your strengths and your secret sauce. Although doing something that you love every day is not always possible, it is a good goal.

MANAGE YOUR TASKS

Time-management challenges are incessant and never ending. In many jobs, there is minimal data on how long the actual tasks take. Therefore, the time allotted is often inadequate, and staff and leaders alike are constantly playing catch-up as they attempt to complete, manage, and balance work tasks. Implementing strategies to manage your time and tasks efficiently is critical to your effectiveness and satisfaction.

Embrace Automatic Systems

The more structures you have on autopilot, the more discretionary time you will have for leading, developing, and setting strategic direction. Keep a master list. You can choose from various methods, e.g., you can keep your master list on one piece of paper, use the "task" tool on your computer program, post your list on a white board, carry a notebook with your master list and supporting notes. Choose a method that is right for you, and then build time in each day to scan and update your list—and cross some of those suckers off!

Skip Email in the Morning

Protect a bit of time each morning to plan your day rather than react to others' issues and fires. You can consider stating in your email signature the times of day you check email. People then get accustomed to knowing your schedule and when they might anticipate a response from you.

Manage Your Meetings

Consider whether you need to be at all the meetings you attend. Are there meetings that, if delegated, can help your team members grow? If yes, let those meetings go. Put a system in place that allows you to receive the critical information and decisions discussed in the meeting.

Even when you need to attend a meeting on behalf of your team, you might not need to be there for its entirety. Set the expectation that you'll be there for the first part of the meeting and leave the summary, next steps, and scheduling to a deputy.

Ensure every meeting has an agenda, distributed in advance, that includes room for discussion of the one or two most important topics. Consider scheduling meetings in 15-, 30-, 45-, or 60-minute increments.

Reduce Interruptions

We allow ourselves to be interrupted for many reasons: we don't want to be rude; we feel we must always be available; we enjoy socializing; and often, we know the answer to others' questions or dilemmas. Clearly inform others when you are available and when you are not, by protecting your calendar, scheduling blocked project time on your calendar, and again, stating in your email signature the times of day you are available to respond to emails and inquiries. Allow yourself to move to a different location to complete project work. Cal Newport's book *Deep Work* has great suggestions on creating systems to protect your "deep work" time.

Managing yourself as you make the shift from doer to leader requires continuous adaptation. Try out the strategies described in this chapter, adapting as your role, the demands of the marketplace, and/or your team changes.

COOKING IT UP: RECIPE FOR MOVING FROM SOUS CHEF TO EXECUTIVE CHEF!

Mise en Place—Shifting to a Leadership Mindset

Reflect on the following:

- How have you shifted your personal identity from a doer to a leader? In what ways do you think of yourself differently?
- Note how you prioritize what you do in a day. How do you set priorities differently now that you are in a leadership role?
- List three ways you have reconfigured your responsibility by reassigning tasks you formerly did yourself.
- Identify an example of how you can elevate your contributions to the organization from your vantage point as a leader.

Step #1: Identify Successful Practices You Already Have in Place

Complete the following self-assessment on "Managing Myself."

MANAGING MYSELF		
Technique/Action Step	Consistency and Effectiveness (assign a number 1-5, 5 highest)	What I Will Do/ Steps I Will Take
Managing My Mood		
1. Start my day with activities that set a positive tone		
2. Regularly use mindfulness practices		
3. Consciously develop qualities of a positive mindset, e.g., optimism, gratitude, acceptance		

MANAGING MYSELF (CONT'D)		
Technique/Action Step	Consistency and Effectiveness (assign a number 1-5, 5 highest)	What I Will Do/ Steps I Will Take
Managing My Energy		
4. Know my "prime time" of day		
5. Use "in the moment" practices, e.g., breathe, move, count to ten, smile, and laugh		
6. Implement "daily" practices: e.g., eat well, relax, mentally recharge		
7. Use "ongoing practices:" e.g., strategic thinking, self-talk, trusted confidante, positive visualization		
Managing My Priorities		
8. Use the Prioritization Matrix or a similar tool regularly		
9. Make decisions daily on what I should keep and when I should say "no"		
10. Define my goals in the evening or early morning daily		
Managing My Time		
11. Manage my meeting attendance and involvement effectively		
12. Manage my email effectively		
13. Take steps to reduce interruptions		
14. Use a system for managing tasks and filing		
15. Continuously adapt my methods as needed		

Step #2: Use Habits that Support Your Effective Leadership

You have the ingredients for supporting your transition and a good sense of the shifts needed to support it. You have completed the inventory of what you have in place, as well as where gaps are, and what is most important to your role. Use the information from Step #1 to summarize the action steps you will take:

ACTION STEPS TO TAKE		
Habits to Manage Myself	Habits	Technology or Other Support
Habits I Already Do	1.	
	2.	
	3.	
Development— Habits I Want to Build	1.	
	2.	
	3.	

 Step #3: Start with Gratitude

Implement the "Three Good Things" gratitude exercise described on page 67:

❦ Every night before bed, take time to reflect back on your day.
❦ Think of three specific things that went well for you during the day.
❦ Write those three things down. Reflect on each of them.

To get the most out of this exercise, be sure to do the following:

❦ Commit to a timeline.
❦ Write your three things down.
❦ Reflect on what you did to get a positive outcome.

Add Your Secret Sauce

Your secret sauce can be a great energizer to assist you in managing your mood, energy, priorities, and time. Just as soothing music can help you feel calm, upbeat music can fuel a workout! Have a hobby you need to make time for? Great, it will require you to think more carefully about scheduling so that you can fit into your week or day. Use your sauce to spice things up as you learn and adapt effective habits that support your leadership. Note these on a separate piece of paper.

Tastings—Tidbits for Your Team

Every behavior shift and improvement you model for your team members in managing yourself, your energy, your priorities, and your time sends a message that this is important for you and for each of them.

- ⚜ **Announce yourself to your team.** Have an honest conversation with your team about the shift you are making from doer to leader and the impact this will have as you delegate and involve them more.
- ⚜ **Display optimism.** Notice and remark on your coworkers' positive behaviors and their strengths. This is particularly important in a virtual environment where it can be more difficult to convey. Take time to compliment team members on things you appreciate and encourage them to do the same with one another.
- ⚜ **Demonstrate positivity.** Start meetings with a recap of wins, accomplishments, and successes. Request that negative remarks and complaining be replaced with broader thinking that allows for requests, solutions, and creative alternatives. Again, this is especially important when working virtually and with geographically dispersed teams.
- ⚜ **Have conversations about prioritization regularly in both individual and team meetings.** Ask for volunteers to find technical solutions to help in prioritization, like apps and project management software programs.
- ⚜ **Encourage self-care.** Provide resources to assist your team in managing themselves, their priorities, and their tasks. Encourage them to share resources such as books, articles, blogs, and TED Talks on these topics and reinforce a growth mindset.

Chop! Chop! Chop!
Getting Things Done Through Others

Stephen Covey, in his classic on leadership effectiveness, *The Seven Habits of Highly Effective People*, describes "Habit #4, Think Win/Win" as: "The habit of interpersonal leadership . . . [is one] that requires the vision, the proactive initiative and the security, guidance, wisdom, and power that come from principle-centered personal leadership." In other words, the leader uses his or her influence to provide guidance, assurance, and clear expectations for the team members. The five elements of win/win that Covey describes are:

- ♥ **Desired results.** Identify what is to be done and when.
- ♥ **Guidelines.** Specify the parameters (principles, policies, etc.) within which results are to be accomplished.
- ♥ **Resources.** Identify the financial, technical, or organizational support available to help accomplish the results.
- ♥ **Accountability.** Set up the standards of performance and the time of evaluation.
- ♥ **Consequences.** Specify what will happen as a result of the evaluation.

Alex, the director of communications and marketing introduced in Chapter 4, worked hard on his transition from doer to leader. As he made this shift and observed how he was getting work done, he described his work life as a tennis match: volleying the balls coming at him incessantly, including emails, calls, meetings, and deadlines. Alex began to evaluate his role by asking key questions: What were his most important responsibilities, and who could he count on to do what? How could he be assured that his team members would deliver on their responsibilities effectively?

75

The style of managing his life and work that had worked in the past—handling most things himself—was no longer sustainable. It became clear to Alex that, along with managing his mood and his energy, he needed to change some habits in the way he was making decisions about work.

Alex had a strong reaction when I brought up the idea that he could delegate more. "I have tried that! I might as well just do it myself. I tell my staff members what to do and when the deadline is, and they either miss the deadline and ignore me or send something shoddy at the last minute. I am done hounding them. So, for the time being, I have given up. I have my own deadlines to meet!"

Following his rant, Alex was a bit sheepish, acknowledging his frustration. He knew he was part of the problem by not taking the time to fully explain to his staff members, many of whom lacked experience, what the work and tasks required.

I asked Alex what he did when the work showed up as less than satisfactory. He admitted that he typically completed the work himself, which explained his late nights and weekends of work.

As was the case with Alex, you most likely can think of situations where goals were set and agreements made, and despite these promises, people did not deliver, and the project stalled, or you pushed yourself into high gear and did the work yourself. That is where good leadership comes in—figuring out how to help others deliver on their responsibilities, so that projects can move ahead effectively and efficiently.

DELEGATION AND BUILDING CAPACITY

Contrary to what some believe, delegation is not dumping work that you do not want or have time to do on others and letting them sink or swim. Delegation is the strategy and accompanying processes and habits that assure the work gets done, capacity is built to take on more, and people grow as they try new tasks and master new skills.

Effective delegation is actually motivating because most people naturally seek additional responsibility. Added responsibility, along with recognition for their efforts, is particularly important for millennials and individuals of Generation Z. Often, Generation Z staff are social learners who prefer to learn by doing, applying innovation as they collaborate with others to find new ways of accomplishing work. Delegation provides a structured method to do this. And as you delegate to others, opportunities arise for you to create and envision fresh ideas: new solutions to problems, new products, new ideas, and inventions.

Delegation requires a different mindset about how work gets done, supported by new habits and processes. When done right, delegation produces positive outcomes, reducing frustration. Team members are empowered and set up for success and capacity expands, so that the team achieves more than one person can do on his or her own.

It's tempting to delegate only to top performers who already have the skills and motivation to accomplish the work without much intervention. Who doesn't find this easy route appealing? But, remember that delegation is as much about helping people grow and learn new skills as it is completing tasks.

The following guidelines can help you smoothly transition to using delegation effectively:

- **Devote time.** Schedule time and energy to consistently give direction. Test your assumptions about what a person taking on a new task already knows. Build in time to ask questions and have a dialogue to figure out whether the individual needs to be shown, taught, or just assigned.
- **Monitor progress appropriately.** Determine in advance how often and how best to check on how your delegatee is doing, as well as how you are doing with delegating. Clarify the approach up front, stay connected to progress, and celebrate wins!
- **Give people freedom to perform.** Give clear direction and get out of the way. Micromanaging disempowers people, slows progress, and hampers creativity and innovation. Checking in too much, correcting tiny details, and taking over tasks before they are finished are all examples of micromanaging. People are more motivated when they can perform tasks in their own way and correct their own mistakes, which makes them feel empowered, energized, and confident.
- **Set stretch goals.** Research indicates that challenging goals actively encourage people to achieve more. Stretch goals motivate people to get out of their comfort zones. Be sure to support your team members in working hard toward higher standards of performance. For most people, it is rewarding to have opportunities to learn, accomplish things, make the most of their skills, and learn new ones.
- **Encourage integration of technology.** Assign team members to engage their peers in finding innovative solutions, as well as ways of learning, that maximize technology. As mentioned, those now entering the workforce are motivated by finding new ways to solve problems, especially using apps and mobile solutions.

❦ **Encourage social learning.** Create ways for team members to support one another as they learn new skills. This not only increases your staff members' capacity, it helps build cohesive teams.

THE WIN/WIN OF ACCOUNTABILITY

Accountability is a mindset and attitude that is essential to productivity. It requires setting goals, engaging the responsible parties, and assuring that the work and tasks are being completed. The win/win of accountability is that both leader and team members enter into an understanding that produces positive results for all involved: clear expectations and timelines promote productive work and allow team members to grow from the experience. It's a mutual agreement on goals and the activities that support those goals, based upon trust and reliability. It involves asking the right questions, engaging everyone in a consistent expectation, and using replicable tools to assure excellence in delivery of work.

Chef Bailey's Secret Sauce:
Teaching Others Your Art

Neall Bailey is the executive chef at Eau Palm Beach Resort & Spa. Born in Vancouver, BC, Chef Neall's love of food began when his father moved from the city and started an organic farm. On the farm, Chef Neall learned to plant and grow vegetables and to care for animals. The pleasure of homemade bread, garden fresh tomatoes, and good Canadian cheddar cemented his appreciation of the simply delicious. His experience as an executive chef includes several five-star properties around the world, notably the Willard in Washington, DC, and the Hotel Eden au Lac in Zurich, Switzerland.

Chef Neall told me about his experience learning from Master Chef Antoine Westermann, the former three-Michelin star chef and the creative force behind the Café Du Parc restaurant at the famed Willard Intercontinental in Washington, DC.

Chef Neall says,

Upon meeting Chef Westermann, you immediately understood why he was a star. His character, grace, and warmth put you completely at ease, even as his culinary skills overwhelmed you. You didn't have to think about what to do, you just followed the star. It was incredible to have that kind of inspirational ideal right in front of you. All of the chefs wanted to be like him.

Chef Westermann told us, "I want you to understand what I'm about, what I think food should taste like, and the direction in which I want to go with Café Du Parc." He went on to personally cook about fourteen courses of the most fantastic, harmonious, and balanced cuisine I have ever experienced. He would say, "Try this, taste this. Do you understand it? This is why these components are combined the way they are." Chef Westermann took the time to personally share the "why" of his cooking so those in his kitchen could more deeply understand his vision.

Until this point, I never truly understood where that line is that separates the truly gifted from others. Growing up in Western Canada, I had never been exposed to a Michelin star standard. I had worked in incredible fine dining rooms, with highly talented chefs. Until meeting Chef Westermann, however, I had no concept of the level of excellence that could be attained. Chef Westermann showed us what is possible in the kitchen and instilled confidence that we could achieve it. It took us to a new realm.

Of course, not everybody is going to be a Michelin star chef. We need to be realistic with ourselves. But you can be the greatest chef in your sphere by understanding what that is and striving to work toward expressing excellence. Cooking at the highest level takes a lot of time, learning, and commitment. It takes a lot of passion.

As a leader, you must find the right people, surround yourself with those looking for excellence and a relationship that will assist both of you to grow beyond the constraints of your current understanding. As a leader and a teacher, you must explain upfront, "This is what the quality looks like, this is what I expect of you, this is what you will get in return for meeting those expectations and accepting no compromises."

THE DELEGATION CONVERSATION

The process of delegation begins with "the delegation conversation," in which two objectives can be accomplished: 1) describing the task/area of responsibility, assigning and assuring the objectives and tasks are understood, and 2) using the conversation as an opportunity to mentor and support the staff member's growth.

I have developed the template below for the delegation conversation. It includes the GROW model, which stands for the steps in a coaching conversation: Goal, Reality, Options, and Way Forward. It was created by Sir John Whitmore and colleagues in the late 1980s and has since become the world's most popular coaching model for problem-solving, goal setting, and performance improvement. I have integrated it with the delegation conversation, describing what needs to be done and specifically what the person agrees to do.

Set a Goal

Describe the goal and agree on an outcome. Explain the context for the task or project and why it is important. This is the nuts-and-bolts stage; you identify who, what, when, where, and how. It is important to engage the staff member, describe the need, and be clear about the expected outcome. Clarify the task on a continuum—how much will get done up front and at the back end—and what the task encompasses. According to Sabina Nawaz, author of the HBR article "For Delegation to Work, It Has to Come with Coaching," you will sometimes need to "Do" at this stage (show how it's done). At other times it will be more appropriate to "Tell" (discuss and explain the task in full).

Look at the Reality

Discuss the current state of the task, where things stand, what the staff member already knows how to do, his or her strengths, and also what the individual needs to learn. Identify potential obstacles and how they might be overcome. Nawaz calls this the "Teach" stage. Explain why you'd like things done a certain way and describe the steps and underlying structure of the task or project.

Discuss the Options

Explore how he or she might do the task or project slightly differently than you would. I love this step because it brings in the richness and creativity of delegation. Discuss action steps and alternatives, their pros and cons. This is where you may need to let go a bit. Nawaz calls this the "Ask" stage and suggests presenting the following question: "What is a key insight from this process that you can carry forward?"

Agree on the Way Forward

Discuss the best path and set clear expectations on the steps, timeline, and how both parties will know the project is finished. (Remember to step back to allow the person to choose his or her own method of task completion. It may be better or more efficient than the way you would do it!) Identify the resources you'll provide, including check-ins, time, and tools, and clarify responsibility and authority. Nawaz calls this the "Support" step, so let the person know you'll support him or her when needed.

Alex agreed to approach delegation with fresh eyes, starting with one project, the website. He identified the key persons responsible, Jonathan and the web team, and would start with a meeting with Jonathan.

Alex and I discussed the advantages of delegating beyond just clearing his plate of a task. These included using the delegation conversation as a way to build trust with

Jonathan, provide opportunity for Jonathan to grow his expertise, and open space and time for Alex to attend to other responsibilities.

Alex held his first delegation meeting with Jonathan, which was enlightening. Jonathan was eager to take on the task, and Alex realized that despite Jonathan's knowledge of web design and some experience in supervision, Jonathan was unclear as to what to do when his team members didn't deliver on time. So, the two talked about how Jonathan could break the work into what the team knew how to do, and what they needed to learn, combining the assignment with motivation for the team members to learn new skills.

The conversation highlighted for both Alex and Jonathan that they needed to "turn up the heat" on their delegation strategies and assure that the team members understood their responsibilities and increased their accountability.

THE DELEGATION CONVERSATION WITH TEAMS

The delegation conversation can be used with teams as well as with individuals. The same questions are asked in team settings as in one-to-one conversations, yet the "Way Forward" step is particularly effective for increasing accountability on teams. (I'll describe team accountability in more depth in Chapter 6.)

Set a Goal—What Do We Want?

Describe the need. Provide context and background. Get buy-in from the team as to the need to take action.

Look at the Reality—Where Are We Now?

Discuss the strengths and positives of the current state of the team. Have a conversation regarding potential obstacles in moving forward.

Discuss the Options—What Could We Do?

Discuss potential actions the team can take. Explore alternative steps.

Agree on the Way Forward—What Will We Do?

Put structures in place and get specific about what each person or sub-group will do, and by when:

❦ **Decide together on the plan.** Then design the steps using SMART Goals for all projects. Introduce the project and the goals. Get in the habit of using the following descriptive language with the team:
  - Specific—exactly what needs to be accomplished
  - Measurable—how it will be determined that it is successful
  - Attainable—how it actually will be done
  - Relevant—the impact it will make, and on whom or what
  - Time bound—the date by which the project and/or sub-tasks need to be done

❦ **Decide on the project lead.** At the front end, decide who will lead the project or do the task by critically assessing the person who has the talent, initiative, the willingness to learn, the ability to grow as they take this on, and who can be trusted to do this well.

❦ **Define roles and responsibilities.** In coordination with the project lead, clearly identify and communicate who is responsible for what. Take questions, clarify issues, and be sure everyone is on the same page.

❦ **Set specific deadlines.** Your SMART goals will include deadlines. Without specific deadlines, tasks will not get done. Be clear when deliverables are due. If they are not met, assess with the team what got off track, and reset reasonable deadlines.

❦ **Document.** Keep a record on paper, spreadsheet, or app of all activity. Engage your team in designing the most streamlined, technically interesting tracking document possible!

❦ **Practice high-impact review.** Implement and encourage your team members to rapidly review projects and provide feedback to the project lead, enabling the project to move toward completion. It is energizing when the project can keep moving and take on momentum!

❦ **Assure accountants and auditors.** These are different people than the project lead. They augment the responsibilities by assuring the task or project is on track with other projects on the team, are reported regularly, become part of the team's overall record of success (e.g., a monthly report, a team meeting agenda item), and meet the standards you have set for the programs and tasks on your team.

❦ **Send alerts, triggers, and notifications.** Ask staff to research and use tracking and project management software. This is a great engagement strategy and also important for keeping the project moving while holding others accountable.

Sending alerts and reminders keeps the project on track and measures the project steps objectively.

ASSURE SUCCESSFUL ACCOUNTABILITY AND DELEGATION

It's important to remember that learning new skills and adopting new mindsets can take time for all involved to develop. And it's worth it! Accountability phases and steps can assist you and your team to keep projects on track, measure progress, identify barriers to success, and assist your team members in taking on new responsibilities. The following guidelines will make it even easier to make delegation and accountability part of the way you routinely do business:

- ✤ **Be honest and transparent.** Accountability is not an exact science, and it takes practice to do it well. Sometimes you'll find yourself swooping in to micromanage; other times the project will fall off your radar. Admit your foibles to your team, get back on track, and move on.
- ✤ **Integrate delegation into what you already do.** Make it part of your process for staff development. Tie delegation to skill building, including the tasks that you have delegated in team members' performance goals. Create mutual accountability for making sure the results are achieved.
- ✤ **Follow the "90 Percent Rule."** A good guideline to remember is that for any given task, 90 percent should be delegated. By giving 90 percent of the tasks to others, you open space and time to lead, problem solve, collaborate with peers in creating new programs and solutions, and mentor and develop your staff.
- ✤ **Involve others in goal setting.** Right from the start, engage your team in setting the goals of any project. You'll get more buy-in and you'll have a more realistic picture of what is feasible.
- ✤ **Assess and adjust your behavior.** Keep a daily diary of how you spend your time and look for patterns, such as time spent on low-leverage activities that can be delegated. Increase your opportunities to empower others. And make time to do so.
- ✤ **Ask others to hold you accountable.** Give staff permission to call you out when you haven't delegated something you should. Be clear you are open to this kind of input. Also invite your team members to take on more; if your direct reports see a project they want to take on, they should request it. And be sure

to consistently invite feedback from your own boss and mentors and ask them to hold you accountable.

♚ **Learn from experience.** Once you have started delegating more, pay attention to results and learn from your mistakes. Note how you can tweak your approach. Can you delegate more often? Give more freedom? Provide more feedback? Tailor your approach to each person.

COOKING IT UP: RECIPE FOR DELEGATION AND DEVELOPMENT!

Mise en Place—The Delegation Mindset

Reflect upon a time when a superior delegated something important to you and you completed it successfully. Reflect on the following questions and jot down the answers on note paper.

♚ What were you asked (or told) to do?
♚ What was the outcome?
♚ How much explanation was given to you?
♚ How much lead time?
♚ How was your activity measured?
♚ How often did your "boss" check in with you?
♚ What resources were given to you to support your effort?
♚ What did you learn? What were you able to do moving forward that you had not known you could do before?

Now reflect on a time when a superior delegated something important to you and it was not delegated or described well.

♚ What were you asked (or told) to do?
♚ What was the outcome?
♚ How much explanation was given to you?
♚ How much lead time?
♚ How was your activity measured?
♚ How often did your "boss" check in with you?

❦ What resources were given to you to support your effort?

❦ What did you learn? What were you able to do moving forward that you had not known you could do before?

Reflect on your answers and circle the ones that were most important to your growth so that you integrate those into your own delegation strategy moving forward.

Step #1: Plan to Delegate and Develop

Think about how you can use delegation to help accomplish your goals and build capacity in your team members.

❦ **Choose the right person.** Note the staff person with whom you'll have a delegation conversation: _____.

❦ **Devote time.** Schedule the day and time to have the delegation conversation, giving yourself time to prepare: _____.

❦ **Monitor progress** appropriately and give people freedom to perform. Determine how you and the staff member keep track of progress. Note how you'll both keep track, and when you'll check in with one another on progress: _____.

❦ **Set stretch goals.** What ultimately do you want this staff person to learn to do and master? How will it benefit him/her? _____.

❦ **Encourage integration of technology.** Note the technology tools or systems that can be utilized for efficiency and motivation: _____.

Step #2: The Delegation "Grow" Conversation

Now use the GROW model to plan your delegation conversation, using the prompts below.

G — Goal
- What do you want?
- Describe the need
- Provide context and background

R — Reality
- Where are you now?
- Positives
- Potential obstacles

O — Options
- What could you do?
- Alternatives
- Potential action steps

W — Way Forward
- What will you do?
- Definitive decision
- Tasks, steps
- Resources

- ❦ **Set a goal.** Describe what the goal will look like, why it is important, and provide the context for why it is important.
- ❦ **Look at the reality.** Discuss the current state of the task, where things stand, what the staff member already knows how to do, his or her strengths, and also what the individual needs to learn. Discuss the potential obstacles and how they might be overcome.
- ❦ **Discuss the options.** This is the opportunity to talk about how the staff person might do it slightly differently than you would do it.
- ❦ **Agree on the way forward.** Discuss the best choice, and set clear expectations on the steps, timeline, and how you'll know it's finished. Discuss the resources you'll provide, including check-ins, time and tools, and clarify responsibility and authority.

Step #3: Use the Delegation Conversation with Teams

Consider your next team project and note how you with "agree on a way forward" using these steps.

- ❦ Identify the project.
- ❦ Draft two or three SMART (Specific, Measurable, Attainable, Relevant, and Time bound) goals to finalize with your team.
- ❦ Decide on a project lead.
- ❦ Define roles and responsibilities to finalize with your team.
- ❦ Set some specific deadlines.
- ❦ Note how you and the team will document your process.
- ❦ Note how you will explain high-impact review to your team.
- ❦ Designate accountants and auditors.
- ❦ Decide how alerts, triggers, and notifications will be sent.

Add Your Secret Sauce

Think about how you might bring your secret sauce to the GROW conversations with your team members. What anecdotes and stories can you tell? What experiences have you had with delegation and accountability that impact how you approach this as leader? What have you learned—humorous or otherwise—that you warn people NOT to do?

Tastings—Tidbits For Your Team

Implementing structured, repeatable approaches to delegation and accountability will assist your team in getting comfortable with knowing that they will be held accountable for delivering what they agreed to do, while also learning new skills. Here are some suggestions for how to keep delegation and accountability on the top of your mind with your team.

- ❦ Discuss delegation with your team and ask them: "What do I do that you could do or help me with? What do I do that you could do with a bit of help from me? What could you do by yourself?" Pick a few things to delegate and try it out.
- ❦ Discuss the delegation conversation model with your team. Get their feedback and input as to how the conversations could be more productive for them. Then agree to use the model repeatedly, as often as you can, so that it becomes a habit.
- ❦ Discuss the accountability steps in the "Way Forward" portion and try using it initially in one project, testing it out, then refining it and using it again.
- ❦ Have the team participate in discussions to assess the team's accountability: "What are we doing well? How can we improve?"
- ❦ Encourage your team members to bring resources and templates to share with the team and try out on different projects.

The Right Cookware . . .
Your Best Team

I love this African proverb: "If you think you're leading and no one is following, you're just taking a walk." It encapsulates the signature leadership question: How do you get people to follow you? And how can you gather people around you that you want, and need, to achieve your vision—to affect the growth and change you seek, for which you are responsible? That, in essence, is the core issue of leadership. And how do you organize people around you to do this? Through teams, of course!

Teams are the essential "ingredient" in how work actually gets done, which is why it is so important to understand the dynamics of teams. Yes, individual achievement is critical, and the organization and culture where teams operate are essential for the infrastructure and mission. But it's at the team level where things actually get done, and it's the team level which holds the most potential for creativity, problem-solving, and excellence in delivery. These things are all fueled by collaboration, encouragement, and human interaction.

As you move forward in this chapter, think about what you already do to bring out the best in your team. How do you engage your team members, how do you propel them to excellence? What do you already know and apply to your team leadership? Keep that in mind as you explore this important ingredient of teams. And now, meet Marc.

In our first coaching session, Marc, the CEO of a retirement community, got right to the point, "My senior leadership team is driving me nuts. Every one of them is talented and experienced, and they are wonderful people. But they come to me individually and complain about one another. We have leadership team meetings, agree to action steps, and then within a day or so, I am getting knocks on my door with complaints about what this person did or that person said. I keep telling them to go back and talk to the person with whom they have the problem, but it doesn't change anything. I've had it—and I need some help!"

Marc had many ingredients for leadership success, including a compelling vision for the retirement community. Marc spoke eloquently of a larger community with more residents that would result in increased revenue. This revenue would support updated state-of-the-art facilities, programming that would interest and delight residents, and services to support residents living independently. Marc confided to me that he wasn't sure his leadership team could actually achieve this vision and manage the growth and change. He certainly had evidence that his leaders were not working together as a cohesive team.

EFFECTIVE TEAMS—THE RIGHT PEOPLE IN THE RIGHT ROLES

Great teams can be built, but it takes honesty and courage. Building a great team begins with assessing the current state, identifying who and what are working well, and who and what need to be changed. In this chapter, I'll discuss the elements that are essential to great teams—trust, the ability to utilize and resolve conflict, commitment, accountability, and measurement.

Jim Collins, in his groundbreaking research and resulting book, *Good to Great*, explained:

> *The executives who ignited the transformation from good to great [in my research] did not first figure out where to drive the bus and then get people to take it there. No, they first got the right people on the bus (and the wrong people off the bus) and then figured out where to drive it . . . If we get the right people on the bus, the right people in the right seats, and the wrong people off the bus, then we'll figure out how to take it someplace great . . . It is important to act courageously and swiftly to assure you have the right people on your team.*

So how do leaders decide if they have the right people on the right team? The right people are ones you enjoy being around and who make your organization better. Those in the right seats are those operating within their areas of greatest skill, strength, and unique ability. Getting the right people in the right seats starts with assessing the strengths and weaknesses of team members. This can be done by utilizing standardized assessments, and there are a variety of those available; however, it first starts with an honest, clear-eyed assessment by you, the leader.

Marc honestly analyzed the constellation of his team to determine whether he had the right people on his bus. There were some assertive personalities on the team, including strong, competent leaders as well as some who had once been, but were no longer, a good fit.

He confided that there were two leaders who had been on the team a long time who were not as effective as he needed them to be. Despite investment in their development, along with his coaching to improve their performance, their departments were consistently underperforming. Marc knew it was past time for him to take action regarding the two poorly functioning leaders on his team, and until now had avoided doing so. As a result, frustration among the other leaders was high, and the vision Marc had for the organization was stalled.

Marc resolved to work with the HR director to 1) restructure these positions to adequately reflect the current responsibilities; 2) compassionately assist these leaders in moving on or accepting lower-level positions within the organization; 3) implement a process to hire leaders in these positions who met the requirements and had the experience needed.

We then looked at how the team was functioning in decision-making and leading the organization as a team. Marc recognized that his team members were acting in silos, rather than approaching the work as a team. We discussed what to do about that by reviewing the elements of successful teams.

THE ELEMENTS OF SUCCESSFUL TEAMS

Researchers at Google studied a wide variety of teams at the company. Their findings about what components are needed for an effective team have been widely published, including in the *New York Times* article of Feb 25, 2016, "What Google Learned From Its Quest to Build the Perfect Team" by Charles Duhigg. The researchers found that what mattered most for effectiveness is less about who is on a team and more about how a team works together. They noticed two behaviors that all the good teams generally shared, regardless of stage, constellation, or talent of the team:

- ♔ Members speak in roughly the same proportion. The researchers described this as "equality in distribution of conversational turn-taking." In other words, when everyone on the team gets a chance to talk, the team does well.

❦ Members, according to the researchers, "all have high average social sensitivity—a fancy way of saying they were skilled at intuiting how others felt based on their tone of voice, their expressions and other nonverbal cues."

❦ Employees on the successful teams at Google talked about how various teams felt and described their enthusiasm for one another's ideas. Joking and having fun also allowed everyone to feel relaxed and energized.

This may seem contradictory with the Collins research noted earlier, but in my experience working with leaders through the years, the two concepts are not contradictory. Collins stresses the need to assure that the right people with the right skills and potential are hired and put in the right roles. I have frequently supported leaders in coming to the realization that a staff member has not grown and adapted to keep up with the changing role. It takes tremendous resolve and courage of a leader to move people out who no longer have the skills or capacity needed for your team.

Google is a company that takes great effort to assure that they have the right people with the right skills and the potential to grow and change over time. Once those people are in place, it is then important to look at setting the conditions for the dynamics mentioned to take place.

Dana Cowin's Secret Sauce: Value Others

Dana Cowin is an American editor, author, and radio show host. An award-winning influencer in the food world, Dana currently hosts the podcast, "Speaking Broadly" on Heritage Radio Network.

Chef Cowin says,

Leading a kitchen can be a challenge. Leaders need to be able to inspire teams with a vision so that every day the team feels that they are part of this mission and make it come to life. Leaders in restaurants have a unique opportunity not only to influence the experience of their staff, but also to impact their community, the supply chain, and the causes they care about through partnerships.

To be a great leader in the restaurant industry, really any industry, you have to be good at a number of different tasks. You not only have to know how to make and serve terrific food, but you also have to understand finance, human resources, marketing, and social media. You have to be articulate in communicating the values of your restaurant, describing every dish to excite customers, the press, and social media. And you need to communicate clearly to your team to show you value each person.

Historically, restaurants have been "No Complain/ No Compassion" zones. For example, if you got a cut during service, you wouldn't go to the emergency room until after your shift. Or, if you were having a hard time in your personal life, you did not discuss that with the chef. Thankfully, the restaurant culture is changing. In today's world, open communication and empathy are as essential to success as prioritizing the mental, physical, and financial health of your team.

I think of restaurants as expressions of love and as places to restore. As a team leader, you need to share your own love and also inspire love in others. You need to communicate your vision so that as team members execute their tasks, many of which are routine, each individual feels he or she is contributing to meaningful work.

CREATING GREAT TEAMS

How are positive team dynamics created? How can leaders be sure that these important aspects become part of the way their teams function? I have been using Patrick Lencioni's *The Five Dysfunctions of a Team* and the corresponding workbook, *Overcoming the Five*

Dysfunctions of a Team, as the basis of my approach with leadership teams and their dynamics for over a decade, adapting the material along the way.

Lencioni designed a fable for the book which illustrates the five dysfunctions many teams display:

- ☙ **Dysfunction 1: Absence of Trust.** Demonstrating an unwillingness to be vulnerable with the group
- ☙ **Dysfunction 2: Fear of Conflict.** Seeking harmony over constructive, passionate debate
- ☙ **Dysfunction 3: Lack of Commitment**. Feigning buy-in for group decisions, creating ambiguity
- ☙ **Dysfunction 4: Avoidance of Accountability.** Ducking the responsibility to call peers out on counterproductive behavior
- ☙ **Dysfunction 5: Inattention to Results.** Focusing on personal success, status, and ego before team success

Because I prefer to approach my work from a positive perspective, I have adapted Lencioni's material into what I call The Five Elements of Successful Teams. I use this material as an essential part of assisting leaders in creating effective teams.

THE FIVE ELEMENTS OF SUCCESSFUL TEAMS

Attention to Results

Accountability to One Another

Commitment to Team

Good Team Conflict

Team Trust

Team Trust

Trust is foundational to teamwork. Without it, the other positive elements of the team cannot be built. Trust is built when team members can rely on one another and when they keep their commitments. It's also built when they can be vulnerable with each other and can admit their weaknesses, failures, and struggles.

Trust is increased when teams learn to take what social psychologists call the "fundamental attribution error" into consideration. This is when we falsely attribute negative behaviors of others to their character while we attribute our own negative behaviors to our environment. For example, when a *team member* fails to meet a deadline, we attribute the behavior to a character defect. When *we* fail to meet a deadline, we attribute the behavior to being too busy or overwhelmed with work. Teams build trust when members agree that everyone is doing the best he or she can, and that if deadlines are not being met, or other tasks are not being done, there is a flaw in the system.

An important ingredient in building trust is ensuring each team member has a voice and the opportunity to talk through challenging situations with the others. As the leader of the team, you can help by making room in meeting agendas for discussion of barriers and frustrations.

Good Team Conflict

A common misconception is that well-functioning teams have little or no conflict. Actually, the opposite is true. Great teams are always at least a little uncomfortable because good team members are direct with one another. Lencioni's "conflict continuum," illustrated below, displays where teams should actually be, right at the intersection of constructive and destructive. Neither mean-spirited personal attacks nor false harmony are useful, but constructive conflict can save time and energy.

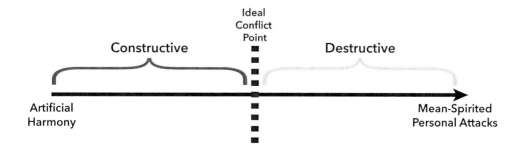

Team members that trust one another are willing to engage in passionate dialogue around issues and decisions that are key to the organization's success. They challenge, disagree, and ask questions of one another, all with the purpose of finding the best solutions.

As the team's leader, you can discuss the importance of team conflict and help the team set rules about how they will manage conflict. You can also "mine for conflict" and ask direct questions about the disagreements.

Commitment to Team

Commitment to the team means that members are willing to put the needs and goals of the team before their own, taking a leap of faith that what is best for the team is best for them individually. Sometimes team members must sacrifice what they believe would be best for their individual careers or for their department's success for the benefit of the team. Often team members believe that, to move forward, every team member has to be in agreement. Commitment requires moving beyond thinking in silos and participating in dialogue that includes all members working to figure out the best way to move forward as a team.

As the leader of the team, you can help build commitment by assuring that important decisions are made after all opinions, ideas, and perspectives are heard. You can also help clarify the decisions by asking, "What exactly have we decided here today?" five minutes before the end of the meeting discussion.

Accountability to One Another

Accountability to one another means that team members are willing to adhere to behaviors that are beneficial for the team. When those behaviors fall short, members are willing to call one another on it. In essence, accountability is each person agreeing to do what they said they would do. It's also calling each other out on behaviors that all have agreed are not helpful to the team, such as failing to be direct, working in silos, or putting one's self interests ahead of the team.

As the leader, you can reinforce accountability by assuring the team has agreed upon their Rules of Engagement, the way they promise to behave with one another. Here are some typical Rules of Engagement:

❦ We put the needs of our customers first.
❦ We consistently show respect to one another.

❦ We call one another out on disrespectful behavior.

❦ We openly discuss issues together.

❦ We ask for help from each other.

You can help by ensuring that meeting agendas are designed to allow for important issues to be discussed, moving away from show-and-tell discussions and allowing time for deeper discussion.

Attention to Results

This final element in the pyramid is positioned well; it's the north star at the top of the pyramid. I can't stress this enough: the true measure of a great team is that it accomplishes the results it sets out to achieve.

The leader can assure that a dashboard is in place that is kept current, assures progress is being tracked regularly, and highlights shortcomings, so the team can readjust as needed. Here is a simple example of a dashboard that leaders and teams have found helpful:

Our Goals and Activities			
Goal	Accomplishments	Next Activities & Responsible Parties	Timeline
Leadership team communication and effective collaboration	• Quarterly Leadership Team Meetings (instituted and ongoing) • Annual Retreat on Strategy and Team	• Continue to address goal setting, accountability, asking for help (All) • Consider the type/method of annual retreat that will work best for team (All)	• Address in quarterly meetings (ongoing this year) • Continue present plan through June
Recruitment & retention of great staff	• Hiring of many great staff • Letting staff go who no longer fit	• Udate workplan to include multi-generational issues (Ana, Marla, Brad)	• Continue to build plan that includes focus on inter-generational issues through calendar year.
Marketing	• Develop multi-year Marketing Strategy to meet or exceed occupancy goals and engage younger residents.	"Everyone is a marketer" workplan—finalize and include: • Transportation to and from key areas • Club House, fitness facility redesign (Albert, Ray, Marla) • Increase class registration and marketing (Marcia, Leeanne, Marc)	• Transportation Plan (by June 30) • Redesign Club House (Sept 30) • Class registration and marketing (ongoing through year)

Successful teams do not happen spontaneously. Building teams with The Five Elements of Successful Teams takes focus, attention, and time, but it will be well worth it, leading to the following results:

- ❦ Heightened self-awareness by participants, as they learn about the elements of successful teams and the role they can play
- ❦ Increased trust among team members and increased ability of the team to discuss issues with candor and authenticity
- ❦ Increased ability by team members to talk openly and honestly and in using conflict skills
- ❦ Increased agreement for accountability, as reflected in the agreed upon Rules of Engagement
- ❦ Agreement upon what success looks like for the team, and a dashboard to measure progress

JUMPSTARTING THE TEAM DEVELOPMENT PROCESS

My experience has shown that building the positive elements of successful teams takes focus and attention. It is very difficult to make significant changes in the course of a busy workday; it is often necessary to embark upon a team development process, and I have found the best format to be a leadership team retreat.

The purpose of a retreat is to help the team members understand the essential elements of successful teams, assist them in building new habits, and demonstrate behaviors that assure they can work together as a coordinated, collaborative unit. Retreats also provide an important demarcation point for teams, which can be referred to as "the line in the sand" moment.

Once these necessary elements are honestly discussed, team members have opportunities to reflect on them, practice direct conversations with one another during the retreat, and make a commitment to this new way of interacting with one another. The team can refer back to the retreat as an event that signifies change, going from the way they once were to a new way of being—there is a before and an after.

If it is not possible to hold a retreat, these discussions can occur in a series of meetings over time, preferably in a concentrated period of time, so that momentum continues between meetings.

USING TEAM ASSESSMENTS AND SURVEYS

Gathering data on the state of the team can greatly assist in building elements of a successful team. The information from team assessments and surveys can be valuable to understanding the current strengths and opportunities for the team, as well as issues that are important to team members. Results can be integrated into the team development process, whether it be a retreat or a series of meetings.

Standardized assessment tools can help team members see differences in workstyles of team members and how the teams can work most effectively together. When teams are not working to their full potential, it's often because the members don't know how to manage the differences in how people approach their work. It is important to help team members see how their responses and approaches may be different than their colleagues'—neither good nor bad, right nor wrong, just different. It's also helpful to assist the team in seeing how opposites can support one another. When team members actively solicit input from those whose styles are different, perspectives are better understood, and collaboration increases. Popular tools include the DISC and the CliftonStrengths. (More options are listed in the Appendix.)

Team surveys can be done through online tools, e.g., Survey Monkey, or ones the team creates. Team surveys request participant input on the strengths of the team, challenges to the team, and topics they'd like to see addressed at the retreat. This information can can then be shared and discussed during the team development discussions.

———————————————————

Marc took the steps necessary to move the two members who were not effective out of their roles, merged two departments together under one leader, and promoted a manager from within to a leadership position on a team.

Marc and I then agreed that the next step in most efficiently and effectively jump-starting his team's use of the essential elements was to hold a leadership team retreat. We designed an agenda together.

The first part of the retreat focused on getting everyone in the mindset for the day—getting to know one another better, building trust, and getting buy-in for Marc's vision for the future:

❧ **Welcome the team.** Marc greeted the team, presented his goals and hopes for the retreat, and reviewed the logistics for the day-long meeting.

- ✤ **Break the ice.** Two team members facilitated an opening activity, which got everyone on their feet and laughing. (Note: see Appendix for suggested Ice Breakers.)
- ✤ **Vision for the future.** Marc presented his heartfelt plan and vision for the organization. He described in detail the need for excellence in all departments, requiring exemplary leadership from the individual leaders and of the leadership team.
- ✤ **Trust building and secret sauce discussions.** Marc and I agreed that it was important to include some time for the team members to know and understand one another on a personal basis in order to build trust. We decided to ask each team member to describe his or her own secret sauce, and how it was important in how that person handled a particularly challenging time in his or her life.

The next portion of the retreat reviewed the information garnered from a pre-retreat survey and the "meat" of the discussion—the five elements of successful teams:

- ✤ **Themes from the pre-work.** The team discussed the results from the survey that had been prepared by two of the team members, revealing key concerns and issues of the leaders.
- ✤ **Five elements of successful teams.** Marc and the team discussed each of the elements in depth—trust, conflict skills, commitment, accountability, and measurement.

Marc used this as an opportunity to convey to the team the importance of having direct conversations with one another about where they were having difficulty and what was challenging for them. He talked about his frustration with team members coming to him individually instead of working things out among themselves or bringing issues to team meetings. He asked the team members to talk about their frustrations and how things could be improved between them. A spirited conversation occurred as they openly discussed the breach of trust that had occurred with missed deadlines and poor communication. This was an important turning point for the team.

Discussions on conflict and commitment helped the team clarify how they would make decisions together and then communicate those decisions to their teams. The team members had an aha moment as they realized that the meetings are where the decisions need to be made, together as a team. They agreed to bring their frustrations and concerns to the meetings, discuss them openly, and get input from one another. They also agreed upon some Rules of Engagement and designed a dashboard for their activities moving forward.

Marc, who loves to play and have fun, used his secret sauce during the retreat. An avid pickle ball player with a wonderful relaxed and informal demeanor, he built time into the retreat for pickle ball lessons following lunch.

The final portion of the day focused on evaluating the current state of the team, agreeing on where they wanted to go next, and what they wanted to accomplish. It concluded with opportunities to show appreciation to one another, celebrate what they had accomplished, and have some fun.

- ♗ **SWOT analysis.** The team discussed the Strengths, Weakness, Opportunities, and Threats of the team.
- ♗ **Design the dashboard.** Using the discussion notes of the day, the team set short- and long-term priorities, and the framework for an action plan. They agreed to the next step of finalizing the action plan at their upcoming team meeting, gathering essential information in the interim.
- ♗ **Celebrate and adjourn.** Marc provided opportunities for members to thank one another and discuss what they had learned and what they planned to do differently. Marc thanked the team members for attending.
- ♗ **Post-retreat dinner.** Marc hosted a relaxing dinner for the team following the retreat, where they could unwind and socialize. This infusion of play and fun added a wonderful dimension and put his team at ease, and they appreciated his generosity.

Marc's team retreat was very successful. By the end of it, the team members knew and bought into Marc's vision for the organization and the team. They realized that they could talk openly with one another about the challenges of the work. They designed a clear roadmap for their goals and activities. They laughed, had fun, and celebrated all they had achieved so far.

BUILDING SUCCESSFUL VIRTUAL TEAMS

During the COVID-19 pandemic, many teams moved quickly to meeting virtually in online platforms. It appears that this medium is here permanently, and that many teams will continue meeting in a virtual format. A blend of meeting in person and virtually may be on the horizon for many organizations as well. The elements of successful teams are as important when teams meet virtually as when they meet in person.

As you most likely have experienced, the virtual medium brings some advantages, including ease of meeting online, higher levels of participation of dispersed teams, and the opportunity for more spontaneity, as participants can often "jump online" for a brief conversation as needed. The disadvantages, which many teams now are working to overcome, are primarily constraints on building trust between team members. Here are some suggestions for leading virtual teams:

- **Focus intentionally on building trust and building relationships.** Designate the first part of the meeting to connect and catch up with one another. Encourage people to show up early and convene.
- **Support the team's effectiveness through technology.** Establish communication channels, including the right technological tools for specific purposes, e.g., how your group will use Facebook. Publish and disseminate agendas for meetings ahead of time and allow participants to contribute to the agenda.
- **Use video.** It's easier to build trust when people can see one another.
- **Assure accountability.** Set clear goals, targets, and use effective and efficient reporting systems.
- **Harness the power of the team.** Encourage teamwork and collaboration, including sub-team meetings and open-ended social time online. Consider finding projects that the team can work on outside of work to contribute to the community. Be intentional about building structures for socializing. Remember that it takes extra effort and time to build a sense of team virtually.

COOKING IT UP:
RECIPE FOR YOUR BEST TEAM!

Mise en Place—Your Best Team Mindset

Developing a great leadership team takes courage and vision. It means taking stock of where you are now and where you want to go. It means embracing possibilities and facing challenges truthfully. It also means knowing and articulating your vision for yourself and your team, and having optimism and confidence that you can take the team there.

Take some paper and jot your notes for each question:

- Where do you want yourself, your team, and your organization to be in five years? Refer back to your vision from Chapter 1.
- What are your team strengths as you see them?
- What behaviors/weaknesses are getting in the way or slowing down the team's progress?
- What do you know you need to do to help the team be successful toward that vision?

This is where you are. You now have the basic components in place to move forward. Okay, let's go!

Step #1: Assess Your Team—Right People, Right Seats

It's important to do an honest assessment of your current team. Reflect and then complete the following:

1. List the strong members on your team, the ones who manage their areas well and bring energy to the work: _____.
2. This next one gets a bit harder. List the team members whose performance is mediocre: _____.
3. List here some action steps that you can take to assist team members from question #2 in using their strengths and addressing areas for needed improvement:_____.

4. Here's the hardest one to answer. Note who is not pulling his or her weight, with whom you, or other members of the team, have been struggling with: _____
_____.

5. State the next step you will take in addressing the challenges of #4 to move toward having the right people in the right roles: _____
_____.

 Step #2: Evaluate Your Team's Success Elements

How strong is your team in the following elements? Where does the team need to improve? Your leadership can make a huge impact in building these elements. Note in the table below the steps you will take to build each element:

BUILDING TEAM ELEMENTS		
Team Element	**Rate Team on Scale of 1–5** (5 highest)	**Leadership Step to Increase Team Effectiveness**
Team Trust—How vulnerable and honest are they with one another? Do they allow everyone to have a voice? Do they show empathy?		
Good Team Conflict—Where are they on the conflict continuum? False harmony? Mean-spirited attacks? How far are they from the ideal conflict point?		
Commitment to the Team—How well do they talk over issues and then come to an agreement to proceed? How comfortable are they in discussing and then moving forward, even when they don't totally agree?		
Accountability to One Another—How willing is your team to call one another out on behaviors that are not helpful to the team? In what ways have they agreed to work with one another?		
Attention to Results—What metrics and dashboards do you have in place to measure your team's goals? How does your team know when they have achieved success?		

Step #3: Jumpstart the Team Development Process

Create a schedule to implement activities that get the team development process going, using several or all of these activities:

- ♥ Schedule a retreat or series of meetings to discuss the elements of successful teams and how your team is applying them on an ongoing basis.
- ♥ Do a team assessment with your team, e.g., the DISC assessment (see Appendix for suggestions).
- ♥ Ask one to two team members to design a draft of a survey for the team to assess what is working on the team and what can be improved.
- ♥ Review and hone the draft with the team and then assure it is implemented. Use the results to assist in identifying strengths and opportunities for team development.

Add Your Secret Sauce

Pushing your team toward excellence takes energy, time, and persistence. You'll need all the secret sauce you can muster! Note ways that you can add your secret sauce when interacting with your team to build trust, resolve conflict, and increase accountability to one another and to get results. What sauce will you bring to spice things up?

Tastings—Tidbits for Your Team

The most effective way to increase effectiveness in the way your team works together is to introduce The Five Elements of Successful Teams, discuss together how your team can apply them, and then keep the discussion going on a regular basis. Here are some ways to do that:

- ♥ Discuss and finalize the Rules of Engagement with your team (refer to pages 96-97 for examples). Review them regularly. Consider creating a poster and/or screen saver!
- ♥ On a quarterly basis, review the team's dashboard and recalibrate goals and activities as needed.
- ♥ On a regular basis, discuss how each of the team members bring his or her secret sauce to the team.

❦ Encourage the team members to contribute additional resources on team effectiveness including books, articles, blogs, and TED Talks.

❦ Encourage your team members to find technical solutions for sustaining positive behaviors, such as apps and websites.

Ingredient #7

Hot Tamales!
Dealing with Difficult People

I bet I hooked you with "Hot Tamales," right? I am sure some specific people come to mind. Difficult people, or hot tamales, can stop us in our tracks. Just like biting into a hot pepper, the discomfort can be all-consuming. When you're seeing red, it's hard to think of anything else. Difficult people can distract you and throw you off your game.

You cannot do much about difficult people. You can try to ignore them. You can try to fire them, but if they leave you might miss out on some of their helpful attributes and contributions. The truth is that at some point you have to address difficult behavior. Note the difference in language. The *person* is different from the *behavior*. And therein lies your power. As a leader, you have immense opportunities to shape the behavior of others, using your role, your influence, your good will, and your good intent.

So, let's shift from the person to the behaviors that get in the way of their effectiveness.

An A-list of hot tamales you might recognize is on the following page. The left column labels the type of individual: blamer, know-it-all, whiner, passive-aggressive, clueless, and obstreperous. Chances are you can identify their behavior from the names. The right column describes the behavior.

| IDENTIFYING NEGATIVE TYPES AND BEHAVIORS ||
Hot Tamales	Negative Behavior
Blamer: It's your fault, or someone else's	Lack of acceptance of responsibility or ownership of mistakes
Know-It-All: Opinionated; you can't tell this person anything; he or she has been there, done that	Lack of willingness to accept input or feedback
Whiner: Constant complainer; sees the glass half-empty (if that)	Lack of action for improvement; more talk than action
Passive-aggressive: Tells you one thing to your face, then undermines you behind your back	Lack of directness; overuses sarcasm
Clueless: No matter how many times you tell them, they just don't get it	Lack of behavioral change, despite repeated conversations
Obstreperous: Difficult, argumentative	Unwillingness to resolve conflict

Notice a shift in your reaction as you read the left column and then the right. Framing a behavior, rather than characterizing a person's character, opens up the possibility for change and improvement.

The ability to deal successfully with difficult behaviors in the workplace is a leadership fundamental. When ineffective behaviors are left unchecked, they have a negative impact on the team, and trust with the difficult person is often diminished. These types of behavior tend to be chronic and consistent when left unaddressed. They can sap your energy, distract you from your goals, and reduce the effectiveness of your team. They can also derail careers of people who are also brilliant, creative, and significant contributors.

As a leader, you have the opportunity and responsibility to address these behaviors and support positive change and growth. Additionally, you can work to create a culture that accepts healthy conflict as normal so it doesn't stop you and your team members in their tracks.

You may be thinking, "Wait a minute! I thought we were talking about difficult people, and now you are talking about conflict! What do difficult people have to do with resolving conflict; they just need to change their behavior!"

If you broaden the lens and look at challenging behaviors as ones that are unproductive and cause conflict, you can better do something about those behaviors. And, when difficult behaviors are seen through the lens of conflict resolution, these behaviors become ones that you can address in the context of a healthy and productive work environment. Then the potential for significant growth and change becomes possible. Let's meet Angela, a nursing director in a large hospital, and Victor, a seasoned nurse in the department.

Angela was fed up with Victor. A long-term member of the department, Victor had interviewed for Angela's department head job and had not been selected for the position. He continuously made insinuations that if he were in charge, things would be going a lot better. Victor was unrestrained in his complaints about how the department was being managed and consistently complained to whomever would listen.

Victor often disrupted monthly department meetings by raising issues and complaints, many of which were based on allegations he couldn't substantiate. This put Angela on the defensive, endlessly needing to explain and defend herself. Angela often left these meetings feeling frustrated and distraught. Afterward, she spent hours clarifying issues and addressing falsehoods and misinformation with the nurses, correcting misperceptions, and responding to accusatory emails. Angela felt that Victor was disrupting and negatively impacting her leadership, her reputation, her relationships with her team, and other relationships throughout the hospital.

When Angela tried to talk to him directly about his complaints, Victor became defensive and minimized the impact of his behavior. He insisted that he was just trying to make the department better. No matter Angela's approach, Victor refused to admit that he was doing anything wrong. He saw himself as the champion for the nurses and viewed Angela and the unit supervisors as unresponsive and clueless to the needs of both nurses and patients.

Angela was really frustrated and asked me to help her figure out a different way to approach the situation. She wanted Victor to succeed, as he clearly had strengths, talents, and insights. She just didn't want him to be such a pain in the neck. Let's take a look at some strategies for constructively dealing with difficult behaviors:

CAROLYN'S 7 C's FOR WORKING WITH DIFFICULT BEHAVIORS

Through the years, I have come up with a list of action steps to deal with difficult behaviors (and people):

1. **C**hange your questions.
2. Be **c**lear on what needs to change.
3. Find the **c**ourage to stop avoiding conflict.
4. **C**onjure up an image of the person exhibiting the difficult behavior that increases empathy.
5. Utilize the power of **c**onversation.
6. **C**ushion the relationship with diversions and your charm.
7. Create a **c**ulture that productively manages conflict.

Change Your Questions

The first step in addressing difficult behaviors is to shift your questions. In her mighty little book *Change Your Questions, Change Your Life*, Marilee Adams describes moving from the "judger path" to the "learner path" as moving from a position of reactivity and defensiveness to one of open discovery, with the goal of finding solutions. Here are typical questions for each path:

Judger Path
- ❦ What's wrong with me?
- ❦ What's wrong with them?
- ❦ Why is this person so irritating?
- ❦ What did I do to deserve this?
- ❦ Whose fault is it?
- ❦ How can I be in control?

Learner Path
- ❦ What happened?
- ❦ What assumptions am I making?
- ❦ What am I responsible for?
- ❦ What are my choices?

The questions you ask reflect and impact your mindset and, ultimately, your relationships. Moving onto a "learner path" allows you to slow down, get more information, challenge your assumptions, and consider your contributions to the conflict. Asking questions is not condoning bad behavior, it is seeking to understand it and see what you can learn.

Angela and I spent time looking at Victor's behavior, her emotional responses, and what outcomes she wanted moving forward. Angela identified three key things she wanted Victor to do differently: 1) stop going around her back and complaining to the team; 2) engage in direct and beneficial conversations about the issues of concern with her; 3) stop raising havoc in the department meetings.

Angela really wanted to have more constructive conversations with Victor. She realized she needed to engage Victor as an advocate and create a win/win situation for everyone. She truly believed Victor had contributions to make, given his knowledge, expertise, and perspective. Shifting to a strategy of learning, asking questions, and looking at her own responsibility in the situation made sense to Angela and she was willing to try this approach.

② Be Clear on What Needs to Change

Dealing with difficult behavior, particularly patterns of behavior, can be destabilizing. The first step is to focus on the outcome by asking "What do I really want?" or "What do I want for this person?" Have your facts ready, know what you want to say. Once you analyze the situation, you will discover patterns, and you then can plan for them. When less surprised, you can keep your balance.

Identify what skills you want the person to develop. All behaviors and habits can be contextualized as skills that a person can use to help achieve a desired outcome. Turning a conversation into one of skill development, rather than criticism, can bring down emotionality, reduce tension, and provide a path forward for change that the person can see.

Let's look at how Angela identified what needed to change:

IDENTIFYING WHAT NEEDS TO CHANGE

Victor's Frustrating Behaviors	What Angela Needed Victor to Change	Skills for Victor to Develop
• Passive-aggressive—goes behind Angela's back	• Speak concerns directly to Angela	• Direct communication • Deal directly with conflict
• Surprise complaints in team meeting	• No surprises—discuss important issues with Angela before the meeting	• Increase collaboration in problem-solving • Communicate concerns directly
• Emotional outbursts in team meetings	• Present information objectively	• Reduce emotionality • Presentation preparedness

ⓒ③ Find the Courage to Stop Avoiding Conflict

Avoiding conflict is a major contributor in ongoing and unresolved, challenging situations. Conflict can elicit our most primitive responses, our fight-or-flight responses, which leads (understandably) to avoiding the situation. Understanding our responses to conflict and addressing the conflict directly can assist us in moving beyond feeling helpless, trapped, or powerless, to directly taking action instead of avoiding the situation.

Avoidance is often grounded in fears that keep leaders from addressing bad behavior or conflict:

🍇 Confronting the person could make the situation worse.
🍇 The person will reject me.
🍇 The person will start to cry.

🍇 Confronting the behavior might force an outcome for which I am not prepared.
🍇 The person might retaliate against me.
🍇 I could get in trouble for this.

Yes, all of these outcomes are possibilities. However, avoiding taking action is not going to reduce the chances of these things happening; in fact, avoiding the problem often increases the probability of a negative outcome. So, you might as well go ahead and figure out how to address the behavior or conflict.

Ⓒ Conjure Up an Image That Increases Empathy

My early professional years included work as a family therapist in drug and alcohol rehabilitation. In the course of my work, I met Rose, a wonderful leader in Al-Anon. One day, when someone asked how she was able to stay with her husband in the dark years of his abusive drinking, Rose said something I will always remember: "I knew he had a disease, and he was sick. So, when he was drunk, I envisioned him in hospital pajamas."

Rose's secret is to develop empathy, no matter who the person, what the behavior. This is ground zero for effective conflict management. Putting yourself in the other person's shoes, finding common ground, and building a connection on understanding is the key to helping others change for the better

Angela found the courage to confront the situation and be clear on what needed to change. She recognized that she needed to start asking Victor different questions. She realized this was an opportunity to learn from Victor and decided to ask him open-ended questions to try to see things from his perspective. She also tried to put herself in his position and have more empathy for him; he was trying in his own way to make things better for the department, but clearly he had difficulty being direct about it.

Angela also realized that she had done her own share of avoiding, and that the only way to improve this situation was to talk directly with Victor about it. She decided to have a series of conversations with him about increasing his effectiveness on the team. Rather than focus on Victor's negative behavior, Angela decided she would articulate and envision the skills he needed to build to be even more effective. She also made sure the surroundings were pleasant when they met, and to give herself time before each meeting to calm down, be ready to focus on the conversation, and have coffee, tea, donuts, or fresh fruit on hand.

Ⓖ Utilize the Power of Conversation

Replacing the word "confrontation" with "conversation" helps to reduce avoidance. Will conversations over difficult behavior be important and potentially difficult? Absolutely. Productive conversations will discuss the behavior you'd like to see changed, why the change is important to you and to the other person, and how you will support the person in making the change. Such conversations allow us to forge important changes while building trust at the same time.

Conversations like these require that we give the other person our full attention. As you listen carefully, you will likely learn a lot. And hopefully, your employee will be motivated to address problems and seize opportunities. The relationship will be enriched.

As Susan Scott says in the book *Fierce Conversations*, "The conversation is the relationship." Conversations about disagreements are not easy ones to have. However, when you discuss issues causing conflict, you have the opportunity to get to the heart of the issue. Scott provides a template for having a fierce conversation that she calls "Mineral Rights." I have encouraged many leaders and teams to use this template for holding a conversation about sensitive issues:

MINERAL RIGHTS	
Steps in Mineral Rights	**What Angela Said to Victor**
Step 1: Identify your most pressing issue.	"Victor, my most pressing issue is that I want you to talk with me directly about your concerns about the department."
Step 2: Clarify the issue.	"Let me clarify. I don't want to get in the way of your relationships with the nurses in the department. However, I want to hear the issues relating to our department from you, so that I can do something about them."
Step 3: Determine the current impact.	"When you raise issues in department meetings without talking with me first, I am often caught off guard as I don't have the information with me to address the problems. That results in confusion and misinformation, causing more work for all of us."
Step 4: Determine the future implications.	"I am concerned that if this continues the staff will have misperceptions about issues in the department. Also, I believe that your talents, knowledge, and experience could contribute to positive changes in the way we work. I'd really like to see that happen."
Step 5: Examine your personal contribution to this issue.	"I realize that I have not worked hard enough to understand your concerns and I also have not asked for your input on a regular basis. You have a lot of knowledge about this department and have so much to contribute. I have not utilized your experience and perspective as much as I could."

MINERAL RIGHTS (CONT'D)	
Steps in Mineral Rights	**What Angela Said to Victor**
Step 6: Describe the ideal outcome.	"The ideal outcome is that we keep each other apprised and that we are united as a team. We will meet regularly, discuss our mutual concerns, and develop approaches that we can take together."
Step 7a: Commit to action ("I").	"I commit to 1) assuring that we have bi-weekly discussions about your concerns for the next 3 months; and 2) being available by email or phone call for whatever concerns might come up."
Step 7b: Commit to action ("you").	"I want you to commit to meeting with me regularly to have conversations about your concerns and brainstorm solutions together. And I want you to contact me in between meetings as issues arise. Can I count on you to commit to these steps?"

Angela utilized the power of conversation by using the Mineral Rights model in conversation with Victor. Following this Mineral Rights conversation, the meetings with Angela and Victor were a bit rough. Victor was initially evasive, and sometimes did not convey all of the facts of situations. He also tended, at first, to try to cut the conversations short by claiming he was needed in an emergency. Angela continued to remind Victor of how important these conversations were to her and to the effectiveness of the department, genuinely showing her appreciation. Over time, they were able to identify the specific issues on which they could work together, and eventually, these resulted in improvements in the department, which the team appreciated.

⑥ Cushion the Relationship with Diversions and Your Charm

Yes, difficult behaviors are often frustrating, and sometimes even deleterious to your team members' success. Sometimes, however, the behaviors are simply irritating and energy depleting. So do what you can to focus on positive activities.

Stories, games, and laughter work in any setting. Food works well when teams are working together in person. Jokes and funny stories can be invigorating. (See Appendix for a list of some website resources in building virtual team morale.)

Recognizing small achievements, including personal congratulations on a job well-done, upbeat emails, handwritten notes, or small prizes go a long way in boosting morale. Acknowledging birthdays, work anniversaries, and important milestones help reduce tension and boost spirits.

⑦ Create a Culture that Productively Manages Conflict

It is naïve, and frankly, unproductive, to expect that conflict does not or will not exist on your team. If you are not anticipating conflict, disagreements, and different perspectives, you not only stand the chance of being blindsided, but you are missing some great opportunities.

One of the reasons conflict throws people off guard is that they are not expecting it. People respond to change and challenge differently but often predictably. The best predictor of future behavior is past behavior. Most conflict can be predicted and mapped out. The more comfortable you and your team can be in predicting and expecting conflict and challenging behaviors, the more directly and efficiently you can handle them.

As I discussed in Chapter 6, it is important to set expectations about how conflict will be managed. Members of your team often haven't built the skills to effectively expect, manage, and utilize it. So, it is important to build skills and integrate conflict into your team's culture.

Building the habit of exploring differences can expand the way you and your team respond to new opportunities and approach problem-solving. Having ongoing conversations about conflict, setting rules about it, discussing conflict styles, and training are all good conflict practices that can become imbedded in your team culture.

Devote time in your extended meetings or retreats to build skills in conflict resolution. Talk with your team about how you can best discuss disagreements or conflicting points of view. Remind them that a healthy culture is one that invites and accepts diverse opinions and perspectives. Training in conflict skills can help staff become more comfortable in dealing with disputes, and in looking for win/win outcomes. Conflict can then be seen as leading to positive outcomes, including better understanding of others or a better solution to a workplace problem.

Angela realized, as she worked with Victor to change his behaviors, she also had some opportunities to create a greater sense of esprit de corps with her team. The department meetings, which historically had been gripe sessions for Victor and others, were an opportunity for her to showcase her secret sauce, her sense of fun. Moving forward, she wanted to be sure there was time on the agenda for funny stories or anecdotes, so she engaged a group of nurses from the team as the "fun" team. They gathered funny videos, stories, and jokes to liven up the meetings. Additionally, Angela used the last meeting of the month to celebrate team member birthdays, where she honored each with a card and gave a brief testimonial to the team noting that person's unique contributions. Gradually, the team meetings became ones that energized the group. Using the 7 C's as a guideline for working with Victor and the team, Angela eventually was able to engage Victor in a working relationship that was effective.

Chef Becker's Secret Sauce:
Seeing Uniqueness in Others

Mark Becker has recently retired from the role of corporate chef at the headquarters of CVS, where he led a team to provide in-house dining at the corporate campus for twenty-eight years. With a degree in marketing and management, Becker's career has included managing the back and front of the house in restaurants, banquet facilities, food services for school districts, and concessions at Penn State Beaver Stadium. He ultimately landed with Compass Group, the largest food service contractor in the world. Becker's varied career has included some interesting experiences with managing conflict! Chef Becker says,

> I was taught years ago that you're only as good as your team. You're only as good as every link in the chain. Your coworkers might have different backgrounds, educations, and life experiences; you have to respect and draw from that. The key is identifying everybody's gifts—their secret sauces—and figuring out how to combine those gifts into something delicious and beautiful. You take what you can from everybody and show them all a vision of the final product. I try to do a good job of making sure everybody feels understood and that their participation and input is

important and recognized. Part of my secret sauce is that I am approachable, even though I am a shy person.

No matter who you have on your team, you will always have conflict. For example, somebody might arrive in a bad mood or may be struggling with personal issues. These things spill into the kitchen.

Communication is definitely essential in resolving conflict. It is important to gather all the information you can before making a judgment.

As Judge Judy says, "Put on your listening ears." Listen to what everyone has to say; digest the information; and only then come up with a solution. Don't rush the process. Take time to hear what the conflict is about. Then try to make a decision that satisfies all parties and avoids causing resentment.

As a leader, it is important to explain how you came to your decision. Let your team members know that you've heard all sides and why you consider your solution the best outcome for the situation. Let them know that you respect them and their opinions.

COOKING IT UP:
RECIPE FOR USING CONFLICT EFFECTIVELY!

 ***Mise en Place*—Your Conflict Mindset in Dealing with Difficult Behaviors**

Reflect upon how you typically deal with conflict.

- ❦ How comfortable are you with conflict?
- ❦ Do you tend to avoid it?
- ❦ How do you handle conflict in your role as a leader?

Think of a time recently when you have handled it effectively.

❧ What did you do to prepare?

❧ What propelled you to take action?

Think about how you can adjust your mindset as you move forward in incorporating conflict skills.

Step #1: Understand Your Reactions

How well do you deal with "hot tamales?" Here's an opportunity for you to note your reaction to common behaviors. Review each type and note your typical reaction to each one:

IDENTIFYING REACTIONS TO NEGATIVE PEOPLE AND BEHAVIORS		
Hot Tamales	Negative Behavior	My Reaction
Blamer: It's your fault, or someone else's	Refuses to accept responsibility; not able to admit mistakes	
Know-It-All: Opinionated; you can't tell this person anything; and don't even try to correct them; they have been there, done that	Refuses to accept input or feedback; not accountable; controlling	
Whiner: Constant complainer; sees the glass half-empty (if that)	Complains without taking action; may monopolize conversation	
Passive-aggressive: Tells you one thing to your face, then undermines you behind your back	Indirect, doesn't talk directly about issues; may use sarcasm excessively	
Clueless: No matter how many times you tell them, they just don't get it	Does not listen; behavior does not change	
Obstreperous: Difficult, argumentative	Unbending, unyielding	

Step #2: Plan the Conflict Conversation

Reflect upon a situation in which you know you need to address behaviors or conflict and have a fierce conversation. Using the Mineral Rights template from Susan Scott's book *Fierce Conversation*, complete the following to help you plan the conversation:

MINERAL RIGHTS TEMPLATE	
Steps in Mineral Rights	**What I will say to** _____
Step 1: Identify your most pressing issue.	
Step 2: Clarify the issue.	
Step 3: Determine the current impact.	
Step 4: Determine the future implications.	
Step 5: Examine your personal contribution to this issue.	
Step 6: Describe the ideal outcome.	
Step 7: Commit to action.	

 Step #3: Cushion the Relationship with Diversions and Charm

Consider steps you can take to increase a sense of esprit de corps with your team. Choose three of the following and note how you will implement the steps:

❦ Stories, games, and fun:_____

❦ Sending personal notes:_____

❦ Commemorating events:_____

❦ Celebrating with food:_____

❦ Rewarding technology and innovation:_____

❦ Providing flexibility and autonomy:_____

Add Your Secret Sauce

Dealing with difficult behaviors and conflict in the workplace can be exhausting. Your secret sauce can be great for keeping your energy up and reducing tension! Note ways that you can bring your secret sauce to challenging situations.

Tastings—Tidbits for Your Team

Challenging behaviors and conflict do not only affect you, they also affect every member of your team. Increasing skills in conflict resolution and directly addressing issues openly increase productivity and reduce tension. Here are some reminders of how you can help your team become more effective in dealing with conflict:

- ❦ Encourage discussions with your team about conflict. Discuss the 7 C's. Get their input on the best way to address and discuss things on which they don't agree.
- ❦ Have your team take a conflict inventory. Then plan an extended team meeting to discuss the results, and how you as a team can work effectively together.
- ❦ Ask your team how they like to get rewarded, and how they like to have fun. Get their ideas. Assign someone to take the lead on activities.
- ❦ Encourage them to share tools and resources with one another for conflict management, including books, articles, TED Talks, and blogs.

.

Ingredient #8

Pièce de Résistance . . .
Your Leadership Presence!

In sixteenth century England, before modern communication channels, people in the villages would hear through the grapevine that King Henry VIII was coming. Many people didn't know what to expect, having never seen a king before. However, as King Henry and his entourage rode closer and closer to the village, it was pretty darn clear who the king was. Considering the brilliant feathers on his hat, the stunning white horse he rode, and the trumpets announcing his entrance, it was easy to pick him out. Everything about King Henry VIII exuded power and majesty. He didn't have to speak, and often he didn't; he just rode through town, people bowing as he passed by. Henry carried his authority in his dress, his accoutrement, and his stature. No need for words.

Most great chefs know how to use their presence to their advantage, wearing their white coats and chef's hats, greeting customers, and enthusiastically engaging them in interesting conversations about specific foods. When chefs come out of the kitchen, you know it! They use their natural grace, confidence, experience, and love of people and food to fill a room. Suddenly the room seems a little fuller, a little lighter, and more energized. These chefs know how to use not only their gifts and knowledge, but also their role as executive chef.

Chances are you know and admire leadership presence when you see it—but you may not be able to identify its components. Leadership presence is the ability to command a room, express yourself with confidence, and communicate effectively to various audiences. Leaders with executive presence know how to carry themselves with poise and grace.

ALIGNING YOUR LEADERSHIP PRESENCE WITH YOUR ROLE

Your role itself carries authority with it, and I would bet that you could use the authority of your role to even greater benefit. Henry VIII most likely had no problem with this, having been told he was the exalted one (and divine) from an early age. However, many of the leaders with whom I work are unsure how best to utilize the authority of their role and develop their mantle of leadership. They often are not even sure they want to. Your identity as a leader most likely evolved from your personal and professional growth, and therein lies the opportunity for you to hone your presence to match the leader you have now become.

The need for leadership presence was demonstrated dramatically for me when I attended a presentation by a renowned physician and researcher. Dr. "Tom" was a brilliant expert who had just returned from an international meeting where he learned of new medications to slow down the trajectory of dementia. He was presenting on the promising news and exciting possibilities to an audience of donors and collaborators in the field.

Dr. Tom's words, as well as his supporting charts and graphs, were so exciting, at first, that at moments, they literally took my breath away. As one whose mother's dementia was worsening, I found myself taken in by the importance of the information Dr. Tom was presenting. The information was promising news for patients with dementia, their family members, caretakers, funders, and professionals.

But as the presentation continued, my mind started wandering. I struggled to concentrate. As I attempted to focus my attention on the presentation, I sat back and realized that everything about the doctor was . . . gray. Salt and pepper hair, silver-framed glasses, dark gray suit, light gray tie. The light coming in from the window behind him only illuminated the grayness.

Unfortunately, Dr. Tom's presentation delivery added to the monochromatic image. He read from the slides, and his flat, unenthusiastic tone contrasted with the fascinating information he was presenting.

I tried to refocus and force myself to pay attention. Suddenly, I had an aha moment. There was a disconnect between the information being presented and the visual presentation, and, as a result, the impact of his message was diminished. Although Dr. Tom's credentials were impressive and his material important and relevant, his lack of presence along with the lack of alignment with the content, detracted from his message.

I began imagining how Dr. Tom's demeanor could match his delivery, and in so doing, increase his effectiveness. Interesting glasses frames and a contrasting tie would be a good start. Speaking directly to the audience, conveying enthusiasm about the material, and projecting and altering his voice, would keep his audience more engaged (and awake).

I realized that if Dr. Tom's external presence matched his internal message, the impact of his words would multiply many times over! And the steps he needed to increase that effectiveness were not that hard—pay a bit more attention to external demeanor and vocal tone, align it with the important information, and wow!

Dr. Tom's story illustrates how a misalignment between a person's words and demeanor creates a dissonance and distraction for the receiver. A famous study by Albert Mehrabian showed that when verbal and nonverbal sources are in conflict, the receiver of the message relies on more than the words spoken to get the overall message. As Mehrabian writes, "When actions contradict words, people rely more heavily on actions to infer another's feelings."

As a leader, you are charged to lead others in positive change. The power and authority of your role need to be reflected not only in the words that you say but also in your unspoken presence. When presence is under utilized, you miss opportunities to influence, engage, and inspire others. And when presence is utilized, you magnify your leadership effectiveness.

Do any of these statements sound familiar to you?

❧ I have never had as much self-confidence as other people do.
❧ It's important what's on the inside, not the outside.
❧ People pay attention to what you say, not how you say it.
❧ I don't see myself as a good presenter—it is just not one of my strengths.

If any of these statements ring true for you, trust me, you are not alone. But also know that leadership presence is something you can build. Think of it as a critical tool in your leadership toolbox. If you are not using your leadership presence and not maximizing your role, you are working harder than you need to.

Chef Flinn's Secret Sauce:
Make Everything Fun

Caterer Jessy Flinn is the owner and executive chef of Gourmet Today, a custom catering company, which she opened in Leesburg, Florida, in November 2011. Her interest in food began in her early twenties when she sought out foods and recipes that would appeal to her husband as he battled a serious illness. Following her husband's recovery, Chef Flinn enrolled in culinary school, and launched the company six months prior to graduating. After ten years of growing a successful catering and events company, Chef Flinn and her team pivoted during the pandemic and added a daily carry-out option, providing breakfasts, lunches, and dinners to her community.

Chef Flinn says,

> Our motto is "rare service well-done." Many catering companies say they offer customized menus, but we really mean it. My friends who were hosting my first catering event said, "Just come up with a menu and surprise us." That's what I did, and they loved it. The feeling of satisfaction was like a drug. There is nothing better than creating custom menus and watching people enjoy eating my food.
>
> My team and I cater all sorts of different custom events and create new dishes for clients regularly. We love catering to a good theme. For example, we did a giant Polar Express for several large corporate clients, including staff dressed as conductors and the food set up on train tracks. We've done The Grinch, luaus, and Grease with poodle skirts. Our kitchen manager is amazing. I tell her, "This is what I'm looking for. Let's have fun!" We have hardcore standards that everyone in our kitchen uses and knows, but just about every day we find something new to do.

Typically, restaurant kitchens are hard places to be. Everybody is hot and sweaty; food is everywhere; and it is rush, rush, rush. The kitchen is an environment ripe for anger and harshness. I was never comfortable in a typical restaurant environment. When I started Gourmet Today, I was determined to create a better environment. If my team was going to spend sixty to eighty hours a week doing something, we were going to do so in a positive environment.

We tell our employees, "This is a spot where you don't have to think about all the drama outside of work, where you can leave it outside and pick it back up on your way out. This is where you can work and be around people who want to see you happy." That positive atmosphere is really important to us. We try to build that family dynamic that lets our employees know that we care about them. We get together after work or catering events to relax together.

We are realistic about the stresses and frustrations of the kitchen. To keep things from "boiling over," I keep marshmallow cannons stocked in my office. When staff members are frustrated, they can walk into the office, grab a marshmallow cannon, and get their emotions out. We also love to play in the rain. In the Florida summers, we go outside and smack around in puddles to let off steam. Sometimes we use the giant sprayers in the kitchen. I always make sure I spray the managers first. You don't have to be crazy to work here, but it helps.

ELEMENTS OF LEADERSHIP PRESENCE

Before I discuss the elements that bolster leadership presence, I want to talk about what leadership presence is NOT:

* It's not about being fashionable or dressing in a particular way. Workplaces exhibit different styles; for example, there are tech companies where even the CEO wears T-shirts and jeans.

❦ It's not about fitting a standardized mold. In fact, effective presence involves laying a foundation so that your individuality and own unique style can be appreciated and valued.

❦ It's also not about being heavy-handed, authoritative, or imposing. Leaders with effective presence embody their roles with grace that empowers others.

There are two schools of thought on how to build leadership presence. The first is to start from the inside out. Leadership presence will then be projected externally by the leader. This implies that leaders must feel confident, then they will project leadership.

The second school of thought is to start from the outside in. It certainly helps to have internal self-confidence, but this second approach is one that regards the elements of leadership presence as skills that can be developed. In so doing, you can project leadership presence by exhibiting its key components: gravitas, effective communication skills, professional appearance, conversational skills, and health and energy.

In my experience helping leaders develop presence, confidence genuinely increases when these elements are developed, even when initially that internal confidence is not very strong. So, I recommend starting from the outside in. That is what this chapter will help you do. Let's take a look at each of these elements of leadership presence:

Gravitas

In ancient Rome, this Latin word, gravitas, was used to describe the bearing of a person in authority. Figuratively, gravitas refers to dignity, authority, confidence, and influence. According to Joel Garfinkle, a highly regarded executive coach and author of the book *Executive Presence*, elements of gravitas include poise, confidence, projecting command, and charisma. Gravitas is displaying confidence and grace across diverse situations.

Leaders with gravitas exhibit decisiveness while consistently conveying integrity. Gravitas results from being self-aware and effectively managing your emotions, thus being able to maintain and manage relationships. Those with gravitas are clear about who they are and what they envision; their confidence shines through in all situations.

Effective Communication Skills

As Sylvia Ann Hewlett succinctly states in *Executive Presence: The Missing Link Between Merit and Success*, "You communicate the authority of a leader through your speaking skills and ability to command a room . . . Your tone of voice, bearing, and body language can also add to—or detract from—your ability to hold your audience's attention, whether you're presenting to a small team or addressing a plenary session of a large conference."

Leaders with good communication skills match their tone with their words, reflecting excitement, calm, urgency—whatever the content demands. They support a strong delivery with good breathing so that others are able to hear and understand them. These leaders convey the importance of their work and message through stories, anecdotes, and examples. Forceful and assertive when necessary, they display humor and banter, especially during tense moments. Their body language is congruent with their words. They demonstrate good skills in speaking and writing, using good grammar and the appropriate tone. They are competent using current technology in communication with large and small groups.

Good communicators are all of the following:

- ❧ **Prepared.** Proactively seek knowledge and strive to stay well-informed. Arrive for meetings organized and ready to engage, having completed background work.
- ❧ **Concise.** Messaging is clear, crisp, and straightforward.
- ❧ **Insightful.** Project their smart thinking and critical analysis. Ask excellent questions and provide great recommendations.
- ❧ **Expressive.** Share thoughts and ideas without hesitation. Display expertise, competence, and talents, creating visibility for their value and impact.

Professional Appearance

In an ideal world, our appearance wouldn't be relevant to our success as leaders, but we live in the real world. It is important to know yourself and celebrate who you are and how you want to show up in the world. I want you to increase your awareness of how your external presence reflects your internal strengths and purpose, while remembering that others form perceptions of your authority through the following elements:

- ❧ **Good posture.** Posture is at the core of the other aspects of appearance, affecting the way clothes look, the ability to maintain eye contact, the ability to breathe deeply for good vocal tone, and most importantly, project confidence. Standing straight and tall, no matter your height, is foundational to leadership presence.

❦ **Demeanor** (dress, grooming, hair, glasses, etc.). Every leader should be able to express the customs and preferences unique to him or her. That said, there are some important recommendations:

- Never compromise on basic hygiene.
- Notice what other leaders in your office and industry are wearing, and if possible, stay within those broad guidelines.
- Incorporate some interest and color into your wardrobe. Find a signature piece. Bow ties, interesting socks, jewelry, and scarves all add visual interest.
- Update your glasses, if you have them, every two years.
- Invest in having your hair cut and styled professionally on a regular basis.

Health and Energy

It is virtually impossible to master other components of leadership presence if you don't manage your health, stress, and energy. As I discussed in Chapter 4—Sous Chef to Executive Chef, this requires exercising regularly, getting enough sleep, engaging in a reflective or meditative process that helps put things in perspective, and doing activities outside of work that you enjoy. It also requires the moment-to-moment actions we take to stay emotionally regulated: counting to ten when frustrated, closing the door and regrouping after a difficult encounter, delaying pressing "send" until taking time to calm down, reading or listening to daily affirmations, reminding ourselves of our priorities, perspectives, and values.

CONVERSATIONAL SKILLS—LEADERSHIP PRESENCE IN ACTION

Your leadership presence is exuded everywhere you go, in meetings with your team, peer and executive and/or board meetings, discussions with your boss, social gatherings, and one-to-one conversations with your staff members—in person and virtually! Here are suggestions for strengthening your leadership presence in whatever setting you find yourself:

❦ **Be present.** Be prepared to contribute to the conversation. Know the issues at hand and the perspectives different participants bring to the table. Arrive early, pick a good seat, and conceal your phone. Be warm and welcoming while displaying the gravitas appropriate to your role.

❦ **Engage effectively.** Listen attentively and demonstrate your interest through your body language, especially through eye contact. Ask questions, don't interrupt, and disagree respectfully. Be thoughtful about how and when to speak. Avoid being a distraction through sidebar conversations, passing notes, or "checking out" when bored. No eye rolling!

❦ **Be realistic about temperaments.** If you are an introvert, there's no need to pretend to be gregarious. Just make sure others know you are fully present and bring your strengths of observation and strategic reflection into conversations and meetings. If you are an extrovert, enjoy one-to-one and group interactions while taking care not to overpower. Don't assume that since someone was present in a meeting, you heard that person's views. Draw out those who tend to hold back. Engage in informal as well as formal conversations.

❦ **Use visual language.** Learn to speak in images, metaphors, and examples. Use charts and graphs to paint a portrait. Speak to people's hearts as well as their eyes.

❦ **Be generous with credit.** Giving credit to others in both private and public settings encourages and motivates everyone around. Celebrate your team members and your team.

❦ **Be authentic.** To quote one of my favorite college professors, "If you don't know the answer to the question, admit it and say you'll find out the answer. Then be sure to do that and report back the next time you see them." In other words, don't make things up on the spot. People see right through that. Rather, build alliances with others who have diverse areas of knowlege and tap them for their expertise when you need it.

❦ **Adapt your leadership presence to various settings.** It is important to be aware of situations in which demonstrating leadership presence is most important. For example, an executive leadership meeting may give you only a few minutes of time to actually speak. What can you do to prepare for this presentation? Be aware of instances when you will have only a brief time to make an impression and proactively prepare. Think about how you can convey your leadership in situations when others are observing you from afar, and how you can use your gravitas, appearance, and demeanor to reflect the amazing leader that you are!

YOUR SECRET SAUCE MAGNIFIES LEADERSHIP PRESENCE

During a tumultuous time in my life, raising a child as a single mother, building my career, and questioning love and life in general, I met Arthur, the boisterous, irreverent, hedonistic food-and-wine loving rector of a large church in my community.

As an Episcopal priest and rector, Arthur had a role that clearly walked into the room before he did. Whether it was the sanctuary, a hospital room, or a casual gathering, people were aware of Arthur. His large presence matched his position. His gravitas, grounded posture, and booming voice aligned with his powerful role, and in so doing, engendered trust. Rather than shy away from his role, Arthur delighted in it and maximized it. I still remember his loud and boisterous singing. No "gray man" there.

What made Arthur special, his secret sauce, was on display most of the time. The twinkle in his eye, his ability to find both humor and humanity in any situation, and his robust appetite for life made him a memorable and endearing leader.

Arthur's magic, the combination of the power of his role, his leadership presence, and his secret sauce, was the ability to make each person feel as if he or she was the most important person, his most valued friend. Through his fixed gaze, rapt attention, and hearty belly laugh, Arthur used his secret sauce to connect. And as a result, people became more of themselves, more confident, when in his presence.

Leadership presence, combined with your secret sauce (in Arthur's case, the twinkle in his eye, his ability to find both humor and humanity in any situation, and his robust appetite for life), results in connection, enlightenment, growth, and a light that others recognize in themselves. With a strong foundation, your secret sauce will set you apart, make you unique and interesting.

Remember that energy and opportunity emerge from alignment. When grounded in your leadership presence, your secret sauce—including your strengths, interests, experience and perspective—can shine. This will turn up the heat on your leadership!

COOKING IT UP:
RECIPE FOR YOUR LEADERSHIP PRESENCE!

Mise en Place—Your Mantle of Leadership Mindset

The first step in honing your leadership presence is to develop a presence mindset. Think of a person in an authoritative role that you admire. It might be a current or former boss, a teacher, or someone in the public eye. Reflect on the following questions:

- ❧ What do I admire in this person, and why? Consider values, behaviors, knowledge, skills and habits.
- ❧ How does this person carry him- or herself? How does he or she exhibit the authority of the role positively? How do people react to this person?
- ❧ How are this person and I similar? What aspects of leadership presence can I increase to be more like him or her?

Consider these questions as well:

- ❧ What do I want to convey about my leadership before I even begin to talk?
- ❧ What is one step I can take to reflect the leadership role that I embody and display my mantle of leadership?

Step #1: Assess Your Leadership Presence

The assessment on the following page provides an opportunity for you to assess the elements of your leadership presence. Think carefully and honestly about the rating of yourself in each element. The goal is to identify two to three elements and behaviors that will assist you in maximizing your leadership effectiveness. (Note: this is not a validated instrument and is to be used for self-reflection only.)

Instructions:

- ❧ Assign a numerical value of one to five (five being the highest) for key variables of leadership presence.
- ❧ Score yourself in each area and note related comments or examples in the right hand column.

❦ Discuss this assessment with a trusted confidante to get another perspective.

❦ Note your top two areas of strength and one to two areas you'd like to develop.

LEADERSHIP PRESENCE SELF-ASSESSMENT		
Presence Aspect	Rate 1-5 (5 highest)	Reflections/Examples
GRAVITAS		
1. Displays poise and grace		
2. Projects confidence and reassurance		
3. Commands attention appropriately		
4. Radiates charisma and charm authentically		
EFFECTIVE COMMUNICATION		
5. Connects with audience/stakeholders		
6. Balances logic with emotion		
7. Expresses thoughts and ideas appropriately		
8. Projects a strong and resonant voice		
PROFESSIONAL APPEARANCE		
9. Displays good posture—stands straight, head high		
10. Conveys good grooming—clean and pressed clothes, hair cut/styled		
11. Projects professional yet personal style in clothing, glasses, accessories		
12. Conveys physical fitness, and attention to health		
CONVERSATIONAL SKILLS		
13. Conveys ability to be "present"		
14. Engages others effectively		
15. Demonstrates good listening skills		
16. Displays authenticity		

Step #2: Adapt Your Leadership Presence to Various Settings

Give some thought to where you leadership presence makes the biggest difference—where the stakes are highest, when it is most important to exhibit leadership presence, and the instances when you only have a brief time to make an impression:

LEADERSHIP PRESENCE IN VARIOUS SETTINGS		
Scenario	Description	How I Will Demonstrate Leadership Presence
Executive meetings	Often you only have five minutes or less to make an impression, and this may be the only time in a week/month that you are seen by higher level executives.	
Running team meetings	What type of meeting is it? What preparation is needed? How can you be most effective in this role?	
Participating in a team meeting	What contributions can you make? How can you best be prepared? What leadership presence elements matter most to your peers?	
Virtual/online presence	What preparation is needed to be most effective in these meetings? What is needed most to get your point across?	
Global presence	What do you need to know ahead of time to be most prepared for this meeting? How can you engender trust and confidence quickly with a diverse audience?	
Walking down the hall	What do you want others to know about you without saying a word? How can you display this?	
Social gatherings	What phrases/questions can you use to break the ice? How can you start conversations gracefully?	
One-to-one development meetings with staff	How can you mentor/develop your team members in the brief moments of the day?	
Other (meetings with clients, customers, etc.)	What can you do to immediately establish your credibility? Quickly establish rapport?	

Step #3: Your Leadership Presence Plan

Now that you have honestly assessed the aspects of your leadership presence and figured out how to use them in various settings, you can capture the aspects you want to work on, the steps you'll take to build those aspects, and how you'll know you're successful. This is a great opportunity to ask a trusted friend or colleague for help, one who can give you honest feedback on how you are doing.

After completing Step #1 and Step #2, note in the table that follows the key aspects of leadership presence that you want to develop, along with the steps you'll take to put them into practice, and how you will know you were successful:

LEADERSHIP PRESENCE DEVELOPMENT PLAN		
Leadership Presence Aspect	Steps I Will Take to Use This Effectively	How I Will Know I Am Successful

Add Your Secret Sauce

Your secret sauce can really turn up the heat on your leadership presence. Don't be afraid to use it. It's what makes you memorable, interesting, and endearing. Once you have those leadership presence fundamentals in place—watch out! You'll be on fire! Note how you'll use your secret sauce to fuel your leadership presence: _____.

Tastings—Tidbits for Your Team

Discussing leadership presence and helping your team members assess it in themselves, will increase the effectiveness of the entire team as well as each individual member:

🍇 Introduce the concept of leadership presence into your team discussions. Discuss how the elements of leadership presence, if improved, could help your team increase its impact in the organization.

🍇 As suggested in the chapter on feedback, Chapter 3—Is This Too Spicy?, start by asking for feedback on your leadership presence in a team meeting.

🍇 Discuss the elements of presence that impact the effectiveness of your team in your particular organization.

🍇 Suggest each team member take a presence assessment. Either 1) the self-assessment in Step #1 of the Cooking It Up section of this chapter, or 2) the Bates Executive Presence Assessment (ExPI), which is the only research-based, scientifically validated assessment to measure executive presence. You can find the ExPITM at bates-communications.com. Have each team member commit to one element of his or her leadership presence to develop.

🍇 Encourage your team members to suggest leadership presence resources, such as books, blogs, TED Talks, and articles.

Time to Start Cooking

I recently placed a call to a local department store where I periodically shop, as a refund for a return had not been attributed to my credit card. After selecting from many annoying options and pressing countless numbers, I was instructed to leave a message. Eventually the general manager of the store called me back. Really!

Over the course of several phone calls in which she gathered the necessary information from me and did some research between calls, I learned she was newly promoted to this job, that this was the third major move in the company she had made in six years, that she grew up in Atlanta, had a dog named Max, and loved the Eileen Fischer brand as much as I do.

We exchanged good and bad stories about the store, and she gave me her word that she was going to turn this store around. I promised I would continue to come back. She offered to buy me lunch the next time I came in. We exchanged emails and phone numbers. I made a new friend. And she guaranteed a loyal customer.

To me, this is gourmet leadership on display—in the department store! Gourmet leadership is taking it up a notch, the leader cooking up a dish of leadership competencies and flavoring it with secret sauce. In the brief but significant conversations I had with this woman, she showed me she cared about my issue, took care of the problem, and bonded with me over shared interests, and in so doing, instilled confidence in me that this was going to be a great place to shop. Her strengths and talents were on display: she was no-nonsense at problem-solving but knew how to quickly build rapport. And as always when strengths are on display, there was energy, momentum, inspiration, and even some fun. Of course, this leader still has to develop her team to embrace her vision and make it a reality. Having interacted with her, I'm confident she will do just that.

I hope that by reading this book you, too, have learned to recognize gourmet leaders when you see them. Most importantly, I hope that you have gained confidence in your own style, knowledge about effective leadership, and techniques to turn up the heat on your secret sauce and put your own gourmet leadership on display.

When you cook up the ingredients for gourmet leadership (also known as fundamentals or competencies) with your secret sauce, you become memorable. People want to follow you, just as I now want to show up and shop in this woman's store. You have had the opportunity to explore how to pair your secret sauce with each ingredient. Your gourmet leadership and secret sauce will delight and inspire your direct reports, your superiors, your peers, and your customers.

Here's an overview the ingredients in the recipe we've explored together, chapter by chapter.

Ingredient #1: Plan the Feast! Your Compelling Vision. Great leaders develop a compelling, clearly articulated vision for success for themselves and their teams. Your vision starts with identifying your personal vision as a leader—what kind of leader you want to be, how you want to lead others, and where you want to take them. From there, follow the guidelines in this chapter to build a strategic vision with the input of your team, clarifying the mission, gathering essential information, composing a vision statement, and designing a work plan to make the vision a reality.

Ingredient #2: Strengths . . . Your Magic Ingredients. Winning leaders take a strength-based approach that identifies and leverages their own strengths and those of others. For you, this is likely to require a shift in thinking from focusing primarily on weaknesses to leading with strengths, including your innate strengths (ones you've had since you can remember) and your manifested strengths (ones you have used and honed over time). Reviewing your strengths in light of agreed-upon leadership competencies helps you to realistically identify which competencies you need to develop.

Ingredient #3: Is This Too Spicy? Feedback and Understanding Perceptions of Your Leadership. Getting and giving feedback is critical to leadership success. Feedback is most effective when delivered in the context of a growth-focused conversation. As a leader, it's your responsibility to create a culture in which feedback is a routine and positive occurrence. Tools and models in this chapter can help you get where you need to go with feedback and growth conversations.

Ingredient #4: Sous Chef to Executive Chef . . . Your Transition from Doer to Leader. One of the most important shifts a leader needs to make is from "doer" to that of leader. The shift needs to happen in mindset, focus, and behavior. Gourmet leaders invest in learning to manage their attention, tasks, habits, moods, and energy. The tools in this chapter can help you manage these elements in yourself.

Ingredient #5: Chop! Chop! Chop! Getting Things Done through Others. Work gets done best when the leader creates a win-win culture of delegation and development of his or her direct reports. Guidelines in this chapter for delegation conversations can help you set clear expectations for results while also supporting the growth of your staff members.

Ingredient #6: The Right Cookware . . . Your Best Team. Elements of successful teams include team trust, good team conflict, commitment to the team, accountability to one another, and attention to results. Gourmet leaders understand these elements and use tools to build them. You might consider using the process for a team retreat described in this chapter. It's complete with objectives, agendas, and action steps to move a team from mediocre to successful.

Ingredient #7: Hot Tamales! Dealing With Difficult People. Although uncomfortable for many of us, conflict, when handled well, is healthy and productive. Gourmet leaders develop cultures that expect and maximize conflict and change, while keeping a cool head when things get hot in the kitchen. As you develop your skill with conflict, consider my 7 C's for working with difficult people, including changing your questions, finding courage to stop avoiding, being clear on what needs to change, and utilizing the power of conversation, reducing the impact of those "hot tamales!"

Ingredient #8: Pièce de Résistance . . . Your Leadership Presence. Your personal asset and tool, as well as your unique style, enables you to delight and inspire others. This chapter helps you identify your own style using a personalized leadership presence assessment tool, including gravitas, effective communication, and professional appearance. It also provides opportunities to link and increase your leadership presence with your secret sauce.

———————————————

Achieving a gourmet level of leadership is not easy, whether you are leading in a restaurant, a hospital, or a company. Because most organizations don't have a standard way of preparing leaders in learning the fundamentals, most likely your leadership skill has been sort of like Swiss cheese. There are also some . . . holes. This book is all about you quickly building leadership skill and becoming the leader you aspire to be.

It's about filling those "Swiss cheese holes" of leadership skill quickly and efficiently. Using the recipes in the Cooking It Up section in each chapter, you were able to apply the concepts to your own challenges and growth.

I encourage you to go back through each ingredient's Cooking It Up section and identify the steps you can take to fill your "Swiss cheese holes." Using a highlighter, identify the four or five most impactful steps that will escalate your leadership right now. For example, perhaps because you are so focused on your responsibilities of the moment, you don't have a clear vision for where you or your team want to go. Or, as we emerge from the pandemic, perhaps a new vision is required, as you and your team adjust to a "new normal." Maybe you are reticent to ask for or to give feedback on a regular basis. Perhaps your team is not functioning as effectively as you believe it could, and you need to focus on strengthening your team by strengthening the elements to help it function more successfully. Perhaps your leadership presence needs some polish (remember: don't be like "gray man!"). This is your opportunity to identify the key steps you can take to fill in those holes effectively and efficiently. Make a list of these most important steps, set a timeline, and make a commitment to yourself to escalate your leadership by filling your holes!

As you identify and apply action steps to your challenges, you'll continue to increase your leadership effectiveness by making conscious decisions about the best ways to lead and achieve your goals. You'll consciously decide how to add your special flavor—your secret sauce—to the day-to-day tasks of leadership, lending your authentic self to the success of your team and your organization.

And what about that secret sauce of yours? You've had the opportunity in each chapter to identify how you could combine your secret sauce with each essential ingredient. Your secret sauce is a combination of your strengths, experiences, passions, and perspectives. It's your unique flavor that sets you apart from others. These different, sometimes quirky, experiences and talents are what make you and your leadership unique. I encourage you to continue to use them, embrace them, own them, and leverage them. In other words, turn up the heat!

When you bring your secret sauce to work, you create energy, interest, variety, and trust. Now that you have identified it, you can continue to be creative, adding interesting, different ways of looking at things, spicing things up, and honing your leadership presence.

This book is about you becoming the most amazing chef you can be in whatever "kitchen" you are in. It is about you finding delight in dishing up your best, in service to others. It's about bringing out the best in your sous chefs, servers, front of the house staff, dishwashers, and bussers. In short, this book is about helping you become the best you can be, so you can bring out the best in your team members. As you bring your best to your role, you ultimately change your team, department, organization, and community for the better, one person, one dish, one project at a time.

Why is this important? Why is it critical for you to be an extraordinary leader using your unique talents, strengths, and interests at the highest level? In short, because your team needs you. Your peers need you. Your community needs you. The world needs you. There are big problems to fix, solutions to find, and creativity to be tapped to create the new.

No matter how talented, a chef cannot run a restaurant alone. Much of what gets done, from food preparation, to serving, to adjusting the lighting in the restaurant, is done by others. That leads us to a basic premise of leadership and this book: your most important job as a leader is to develop others. Whatever your industry, the only way to perform at your highest and negotiate our world of constant change is by developing others.

And the change is certainly upon us. Until the pandemic ends, and until significant movement is made on racial justice, you will be leading your team through continuous change. You will be challenged during this time in ways you most likely never imagined. A talented leader with whom I worked in leadership coaching said, "That leadership plan that we worked on last year was great, and I learned a lot. But I feel like because of these turbulent times, I am having to function at an incredibly high level of performance. I am leading through so many unknowns and challenges. I need to be the best leader I can be at every turn."

Multiple pressures exist for most leaders right now—and will continue to do so. The *Harvard Business Review* article: "Leadership in a Permanent Crisis" by Ronald Heifetz, Alexander Grashow, and Marty Linksy states, "Crisis leadership has two distinct phases. First is that emergency phase when your task is to stabilize the situation and buy time. Second is the adaptive phase, when you tackle the underlying causes of the crisis and build the capacity to thrive in a new reality."

Being a leader at the gourmet level requires the essential ingredients—a clear and compelling vision, using your strengths and the strengths of others, giving, and receiving respectful feedback, assuring you are taking care of yourself and managing your stress, building a successful team, delegating effectively to others, using conflict skills, and displaying leadership presence. It all gets seasoned with your special secret sauce, energizing and engaging others to help you all achieve greatness.

Remember to take care of yourself. This is a time to build resilience. You must rest. It is essential to balance realism with optimism. Find sanctuaries and time for reflection. Reach out to confidants and support one another. And bring on your secret sauce! Bring more of your emotional, wonderful self to the workplace. Stay strong, healthy, and, when possible, joyful.

Gourmet leadership is the combination of skill and creativity that all great head chefs and all great leaders have. It's the ability to inspire, engage, and develop others to get things done the right way, using the excellence, flavor, and style of that individual's unique approach. You have studied and reflected on the ingredients needed to bring these things into whatever kitchen you lead. You've identified your own secret sauce. It's time to start cooking. Don't forget to turn up the heat!

About the Author

A successful communicator, entrepreneur, collaborator, and self-proclaimed "foodie," Carolyn Maue partners with talented leaders to maximize their strengths in motivating their teams to innovate, solve complex problems, and position their organizations for growth. Carolyn's mission to "Change the World One Leader at a Time" is realized through coaching forward-thinking leaders to develop their own "secret sauce" and inspire those around them to be the best they can be. Known for a caring and sophisticated approach that combines leadership theory, practical strategies, and personal experiences,  Carolyn serves up a mix of the perfect ingredients for people to cultivate a leadership style that benefits their aspirations, organizations, and communities. She has 25-plus years of experience leveraging individual and organizational abilities to affect positive change, including leading and developing employee assistance programs and diversity and work-life initiatives. In 2004, Carolyn founded The Maue Center to provide tailored approaches to leadership development and problem-solving challenges for professionals, teams, and organizations. Carolyn also serves as the leadership consultant for the Florida Public Relations Association and is a member of the Alexcel Group, The Alliance for Leadership Excellence. Her interests in international travel, singing, and cooking inform her creative approaches. A semi-proficient baker, Carolyn's favorite way of being described is: "She makes a mean apple pie."

Connect with Carolyn

On the web at **www.gourmetleadershipbook.com** or **www.mauecenter.com**

Via email at **carolyn@gourmetleadershipbook.com**

And on **LinkedIn**

What's Next: The Maue Center

Carolyn Maue and the consultants of The Maue Center serve as trusted resources to leaders in envisioning the future for their organizations and building essential skills, increasing capacity to take on increasing opportunities and challenges. Founded in 2004, The Maue Center works with forward-thinking executives to guide leaders in increasing their effectiveness and using power with wisdom to positively impact their teams, organizations, and communities.

The Maue Center leadership consulting professionals practice the core values on which The Maue Center was founded. These values influence our behaviors, decisions, and practices in working our clients, contractors, and collaborators:

- ❦ Integrity. Goals and intentions are honorable and clear.
- ❦ Clarity. Ideas and issues are presented in concise and objective formats.
- ❦ Development. Conflict is an opportunity for growth.
- ❦ Collaboration. Diverse stakeholders are considered and honored.
- ❦ Kindness. Civility, respect, and graciousness are extended to all.
- ❦ Trust. Integrity, commitment, and follow-through are considered essential.

Carolyn Maue and the consultants of The Maue Center are available to coach you and your leaders, supporting you in envisioning a future and assuring a means to get there. You can contact Carolyn and find additional information on The Maue Center at http://www.mauecenter.com.

For more resources from
Gourmet Leadership: Turn up the heat on your secret sauce!
and downloadable copies of leadership ingredients and recipes go to:
www.gourmetleadershipbook.com

Resources: Suggested Reading, Tools, and Websites

INGREDIENT #1: PLAN THE FEAST! YOUR COMPELLING VISION

Sinek, Simon. *Start with Why: How Great Leaders Inspire Everyone to Take Action*, (New York: Penguin Books, 2011).

Stowell, Steven J., Ph.D. and Stephanie S. Mead, MBA. *The Art of Strategic Leadership: How leaders at All Levels Prepare Themselves, Their Teams, and Organizations for the Future*, (Hoboken: Wiley, 2016).

Watkins, Michael D. *The First Ninety Days: Proven Strategies for Getting UP to Speed Faster and Smarter*, (Boston: Harvard Business Review Press, 2013).

TED Talks

Schwantes, Marcel, "9 Best TED Talks to Help You Become a Better Leader", Inc., https://www.inc.com/marcel-schwantes/first-90-days-ted-talks-to-help-you-become-a-better-leader.html.

INGREDIENT #2: STRENGTHS . . . YOUR MAGIC INGREDIENTS

Cain, Susan. *Quiet: The Power of Introverts in a World That Can't Stop Talking*, (New York: Random House, Inc., 2013).

Parsons, Nancy E. *Women Are Creating the Glass Ceiling and Have the Power to End It*, (New York: WSA Publishing, 2019).

Rath, Tom and Barry Conche. *Strengths Based Leadership*, (New York: Gallup Press, 2008).

Seligman, Martin E.P., Ph.D. *Authentic Happiness: Using the New Positive Psychology to Realize Your Potential for Lasting Fulfillment*, (New York: Free Press, 2002).

Korn Ferry. *FYI: For Your Improvement—Competencies Development Guide*. (Atlanta, GA: Korn Ferry, 2004).

TED Talks

Lopez, Shane. July 18, 2018, Focusing on Your Strengths [Video], TEDxUCCS, https://www.youtube.com/watch?v=tlFPVhfPzNA.

Tools

1. Clifton Strengths Finder—Choose one the following ways to access the assessment:
   - Go to www.gallup.com, sign up and take the assessment. There are several different levels and corresponding prices – the most basic is fine. OR . . .
   - Buy a book: *StrengthsFinders 2.0* or *Strengths Based Leadership*
2. Strengths Profile: https://www.strengthsprofile.com.

INGREDIENT #3: IS THIS TOO SPICY? FEEDBACK AND UNDERSTANDING PERCEPTIONS OF YOUR LEADERSHIP

Carucci, Ron. "4 Ways to Get Truly Honest Feedback From Employees," *Harvard Business Review*, November 23, 2017, https://hbr.org/2017/11/4-ways-to-get-honest-critical-feedback-from-your-employees.

Grenny, Joseph. "A 3-Step Plan for Turning Weaknesses into Strengths," *Harvard Business Review*, January 26, 2017, https://hbr.org/2017/01/a-3-step-plan-for-turning-weaknesses-into-strengths.

Grenny, Joseph. "How to Be Resilient in the Face of Harsh Criticism," *Harvard Business Review*, June 17, 2019, https://hbr.org/2019/06/how-to-be-resilient-in-the-face-of-harsh-criticism.

TED Talks

Hirsch, Joe. December 5, 2018, "The Joy of Getting Feedback" [Video], TEDxTarrytown, https://www.youtube.com/watch?v=h4zNEl7XgXI.

INGREDIENT #4: SOUS CHEF TO EXECUTIVE CHEF . . . YOUR TRANSITION FROM DOER TO LEADER

Allen, David. *Getting Things Done: The Art of Stress-Free Productivity*, (New York: Penguin Group, 2001).

Bradberry, Travis and Jean Greaves. *Emotional Intelligence 2.0*, (San Diego: Talent Smart, Inc., 2009).

Bridges, William. *Managing Transitions: Making the Most of Change* (25th Anniversary Edition), (Boston: Da Capo Lifelong Books, 2017).

Brown, Brené. *Daring Greatly*, (New York: Gotham Books, 2012).

Duhigg, Charles. *The Power of Habit: Why We Do What We Do in Life and Business*, (New York: Random House Trade Paperbacks, 2014).

Loehr, Jim and Tony Schwartz. *The Power of Full Engagement: Managing Energy, Not Time, Is the Key to High Performance and Personal Renewal*, (New York: Free Press, 2005).

Lyubomirsky, Sonja. *The How of Happiness: A New Approach to Getting the Life You Want*, (London: Penguin Books, 2008).

Marston, Ama and Stephanie Marston, "To Handle Increased Stress, Build Your Resilience," *Harvard Business Review*, February 19, 2018, https://hbr.org/2018/02/to-handle-increased-stress-build-your-resilience.

Moss, Jennifer, "Beyond Burned Out," *Harvard Business Review*, February 10, 2021, https://hbr.org/2021/02/beyond-burned-out.

"Three Good Things," *Greater Good in Action*, https://ggia.berkeley.edu/practice/three-good-things.

TED Talks

Briceno, Eduardo. November 18, 2012, "The Power of belief – mindset and belief" [Video], TEDxManhattanBeach, https://www.youtube.com/watch?v=pN34FNbOKXc

INGREDIENT #5: CHOP! CHOP! CHOP! GETTING THINGS DONE THROUGH OTHERS

Buckley, Jared, "12 Principles to Developing Millennial Talent," *Huff Post*, December 13, 2016, https://www.huffpost.com/entry/12-principles-to-developi_b_13538294.

Gallo, Amy, "Why Aren't You Delegating?", *Harvard Business Review*, July 26, 2012, https://hbr.org/2012/07/why-arent-you-delegating.

Kegan, Robert and Lisa Laskow Lahey. *Immunity to Change: How to Overcome It and Unlock the Potential in Yourself and Your Organization*,(Brighton: Harvard Business School Publishing, 2009).

Process for Developing Your People," *MindTools*, https://www.mindtools.com/pages/article/newLDR_89.htm.

Wickman, Gino. *Traction*, (Dallas: BenBella Books, Inc., 2011).

Zander, Rosamund Stone and Benjamin Zander. *The Art of Possibility*, (New York: Penguin Group Inc., 2000).

TED Talks

Hardy, Darren. June 13, 2019, "The Art of Delegation" [Video], TED Conferences, https://www.youtube.com/watch?v=aZK3zS7l848.

INGREDIENT #6: THE RIGHT COOKWARE . . . YOUR BEST TEAM

"24 Virtual Team Building Activities Remote Teams Love in 2021," *Time Doctor*, https://biz30.timedoctor.com/virtual-team-building/.

Aarons-Mele, Morra. "Leading Through Anxiety," *Harvard Business Review*, May 11, 2020, https://hbr.org/2020/05/leading-through-anxiety.

Bariso, Justin. "Google Spent Years Studying Effective Teams. This Single Quality Contributed Most to Their Success," *Inc.,* January 7, 2018, https://www.inc.com/justin-bariso/google-spent-years-studying-effective-teams-this-single-quality-contributed-most-to-their-success.html.

Clay, Cynthia. *Eight Essential Strategies to Lead Virtual Team*, (Bellingham, WA: Net Speed Learning Solutions), https://netspeedlearning.com/resource/virtualleaderchecklist.

Lencioni, Patrick. *The Advantage.* (San Francisco: Jossey-Bass, 2012).

Levin, Lawrence S. *Top Teaming: A Roadmap for Teams Navigating the Now, The New, and The Next*, (Bloomington: iUniverse Publishing, 2011).

Markos, Val, PhD and Tammy Martin. *Player-Coach: How to Shift from Subject Matter Expert to Leader and Getting the Best from the Team*, (Atlanta: Player-Coach Leadership Press, 2019).

Watkins, Michael D. "Making Virtual Teams Work: Ten Basic Principles," *Harvard Business Review.*

TED Talks

Edmondson, Amy. October, 2017, "How to Turn a Group of Strangers into a Team", [Video], TEDSalon, https://www.ted.com/talks/amy_edmondson_how_to_turn_a_group_of_strangers_into_a_team?language=en

Tools

DISC Profile—https://www.discprofile.com/what-is-disc

INGREDIENT #7: HOT TAMALES! DEALING WITH DIFFICULT PEOPLE

Artman Fox, Bonnie, MS, LMFT. *How Did My Family Get in My Office?!*, (Dublin, OH: Telemachus Press, 2020).

Fisher, Roger, William Ury, and Bruce Patton. *Getting to Yes*, (New York: Penguin Group, Inc., 2011).

Patterson, Kerry, Joseph Grenny, Ron McMillan, and Al Switzler. *Crucial Conversations: Tools for Talking When Stakes Are High*, (New York: McGraw Hill, 2002).

Kohlrieser, George. *Hostage at the Table: How Leaders Can Overcome Conflict, Influence Others, and Raise Performance*, (San Francisco: Jossey-Bass, 2006).

TED Talks
Gallo, Amy. November 18, 2019, "The Gift of Conflict," [Video], TEDxBroadway, https://www.youtube.com/watch?v=MnaLS7OE2pk

Tools
Thomas-Kilmann conflict inventory: https://theassessmentsite.com/?gclid=CjwKCAjwi9-HBhACEiwAPzUhHD83TCdvWM-KZtAOs7pQN-myFPMUXCOT5J2fj8Hw_NEGKN1nHFFalRoCBTcQAvD_BwE .

INGREDIENT #8: PIECE DE RESISTANCE . . . YOUR LEADERSHIP PRESENCE

Bacon, Terry R. *Elements of Influence*, (New York: American Management Association, 2012).

Duckworth, Angela. *Grit: The Power of Passion and Perseverance*, (New York: Scribner, 2018).

Eblin, Scott. *The Next Level: What Insiders Know About Executive Success*, (Boston: Nicholas Brealey Publishing, 2011).

Jen Su, Amy and Muriel Maignan Wilkins. *Own the Room*, (Boston: Harvard Business School Publishing, 2013).

"The Mehrabian Myth," *The Successful Presenter*, https://www.presentwithease.com/successful-presenter/files/the-mehrabian-myth.html.

TED Talks

Cuddy, Amy. October 1, 2012,"Your Body Language May Shape Who You Are" [Video], TEDGlobal, https://www.youtube.com/watch?v=Ks-_Mh1QhMc.

Tools

Bates Executive Presence Assessment (EXPI): https://www.bates-communications. com/what-we-do/executive-presence-assessment.